# CANADIAN
# MYSTERIES
## OF THE
# UNEXPLAINED

# CANADIAN MYSTERIES
## OF THE
# UNEXPLAINED

## INVESTIGATIONS INTO THE FANTASTIC, THE BIZARRE AND THE DISTURBING

**JOHN MARLOWE**

ARCTURUS

ARCTURUS

This edition published in 2009 by Arcturus Publishing Limited
26/27 Bickels Yard, 151–153 Bermondsey Street,
London SE1 3HA

ISBN: 978-1-84837-194-1
AD001089EN

Printed in Singapore

# CONTENTS

# INTRODUCTION

To sixteenth-century European explorers, Canada was a great mystery. This immense, uncharted territory was part of a New World populated by mysterious peoples with strange customs, and speaking in unknown languages. It was a land of creatures that they had never before encountered; not even in books. These men returned to Europe with exotic foods, such as potatoes, tomatoes, blueberries and strawberries. In 1536, Jacques Cartier went so far as to bring back – kidnap really – several native people, including Donnacona, the Chief of Stadacona. Presented before the French court, he told François I of many wondrous creatures, including men with bat-like wings who flew to the ground from treetops. More intriguing to the French monarch was Donnacona's description of the Kingdom of the Saguenay, a land rich in gold, silver and rubies, with an abundance of nutmeg, cloves and pepper, at which he would find white men like himself.

We now know Donnacona's stories to be fanciful, perhaps told in the hope that he would be returned to Canada to serve as a guide to this incredible kingdom. It was not to be – he died before Cartier's next voyage.

There were, of course, riches to be found in Canada, and other mysteries to be uncovered. In his search for a passage to Asia, Cartier twice visited Hochelaga, an impressive fortified Iroquois village on the Island of Montreal. As the explorer and his men approached they were greeted by over one thousand people.

Seventy-odd years would pass before 1604, when Europeans again visited Hochelaga. Led by Samuel de Champlain, these men found no trace of what had once been the largest known native settlement in Canada. The tales of the fate of the vanished village probably started then and there. It has been variously argued that its inhabitants died of Old World viruses carried by Cartier and his men, that they were all killed in a war with the Mohawk, or that they simply decided to relocate to the shores of the Great Lakes. There is not even a consensus as to where exactly Hochelaga was located. Four centuries after its disappearance was first recorded, no archaeological remains have been uncovered.

While the mystery of Hochelaga is taught to schoolchildren – just part of the story of the early French explorers and the history of New France – it is perhaps best known to those who live in Montreal. The mysteries featured in this book are all Canadian, but each is likely to be most familiar to those who live in the communities and regions in which they are centred. For the most part, they are stories steeped in regional history.

One of the best examples of this is the story of Ambrose Small. After the unexplained disappearance of this Ontario theatre impresario, his rather unseemly private life was exposed in newspapers across the country. None of these revelations, some of which had been made public by his wife, helped find the missing millionaire, but they did inspire stories that had him enjoying the company of women the world over.

The mystery of Ambrose Small is as fresh as the day he vanished. Over 90 years have passed and we are not a single step closer to determining what happened. The same, however, cannot be said for many of the other mysteries found in this book. The hidden life of Grey Owl, the Englishman who passed himself off as a native of Apache descent, has come to be well documented. The fate of the Franklin

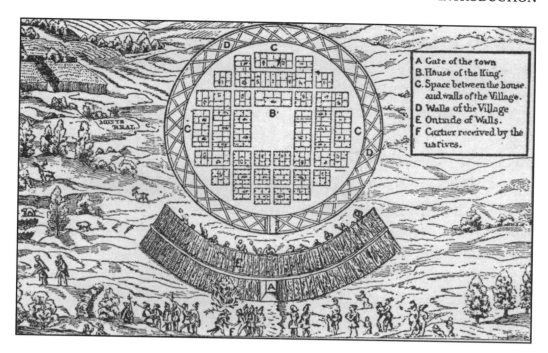

The legend on the image reads:

A Gate of the town.
B. House of the King.
C. Space between the house and walls of the Village.
D Walls of the Village.
E Outside of Walls.
F Cartier received by the natives.

RIGHT : **Hochelaga, as detailed in the first map of any North American settlement.**

Expedition has also become clearer over time. That said, we will never know for certain what came to pass onboard the expedition's two ships: the *Terror* and the *Erebus,* as very few physical remains of the ill-fated expedition have survived.

The dedication demonstrated by Owen Beattie and others involved in the scientific investigations of the lost expedition led to some very significant findings. Not all who have looked into these mysteries have been so rewarded. For more than twenty years the late Don Bell pursued the McGill student who was said to have accidentally killed the escapologist, Houdini, only to find that the man had died decades before the search was begun. In the end, we are left with *The Man Who Killed Houdini*, Bell's highly entertaining and informative account of the chase. Sadly, he did not live to see it published.

Individuals who pursue these mysteries, particularly those that concern things paranormal, crypto-zoological and extraterrestrial, are frequently met with derision. How can one believe in ghosts and lake monsters in the 21st century? And yet, still they persist, sometimes at the risk of their professional reputations. Long may they continue. 'The Northern lights have seen queer sights' and these should be recorded.

Canada's history is found in these stories, from Salish accounts of the monster *N'ha-a-tik* swimming in Lake Okanagan to the UFO that is said to have sunk in Shag Harbour, Nova Scotia. We are exposed to the country's 18th-century justice in the story of the death of *La Corriveau* and the struggles of early immigrants in the Donnelly massacre. We witness the dark days of Duplessis-era Quebec through murderer Wilbert Coffin's execution and we are reminded of the tense atmosphere of the Cold War in the suicide of diplomat E. Herbert Norman. The tragedy of the lost Franklin Expedition serves as one more indication that the Arctic Ocean is changing at an alarming rate. The Northwest Passage, that mysterious passage to Asia that eluded Sir John Franklin, his men, and hundreds of others who followed, becomes easier to sail with each passing year. Mystery hunters now envision a day when the wrecks of the *Terror* and the *Erebus* will be found.

'One learns one's mystery at the price of one's innocence', wrote Robertson Davies. He was the wisest of men.

John Marlowe
Montreal, 2009

# CHAPTER 1:
# CURIOUS CREATURES

# Champlain's Fish and Other Lake Monsters

In *Voyages*, Samuel de Champlain's 1604 chronicle of his encounters in the New World, the explorer describes his visit to the lake he would immodestly name after himself. There, he encountered *charoufarou*, fish that were 'some five feet long, which were as large as my thigh; the head being as big as my two fists, with a snout two feet and a half long, and a double row of very sharp and dangerous teeth'. Historians generally agree that Champlain exaggerated his description, perhaps in the interests of maintaining the flow of funds for his expeditions, and that what he really saw were pike.

Today, four centuries after the explorer first set eyes on Lake Champlain, which today straddles the border between Quebec and New York State, tourists have come to visit the body of water hoping to catch sight of another creature known as 'Champ'.

The first accounts of this monster are found amongst the Iroquois and the Abenaki peoples living around Lake Champlain. The Abenaki called the

ABOVE :
**The waters of Lake Champlain are shared by Quebec, Vermont and New York State.**

ABOVE RIGHT:
**Sailboats on Lake Champlain. Since the late 19th century it has been a popular spot for vacationing.**

OPPOSITE PAGE TOP LEFT :
**A traditional depiction of Samuel de Champlain. In fact, there are no known portraits dating from his lifetime.**

OPPOSITE PAGE : **The placid waters of Lake Champlain.**

monster *tatoskok*, and they described it as a snake-like creature with horns on its head.

The earliest non-native sighting came from a Captain Crum, who in July 1819, spotted the creature some 180 metres (600 feet) from his scow. The captain described the lake monster as being 68 metres (220 feet) in length, black in colour, with a head that resembled a sea horse.

Champ's most active year would appear to have been 1873, beginning when a team of railway workers spotted his head emerging from the water. That July, Nathan H. Mooney, a local sheriff, reported having seen a 'gigantic water serpent' roughly eight metres (25 feet) long, swimming roughly 45 metres (150 feet) from the shore. Sheriff Mooney stated that his proximity to the creature had allowed him to view 'round white spots inside its mouth'.

The month after the sheriff's report, an even more dramatic encounter appears to have taken place. The *W. B. Eddy*, a steamship carrying tourists, nearly capsized when it struck an object that everyone was certain had been the monster.

These incidents, one of which was reported in *The New York Times*, attracted the attention of the savvy showman P. T. Barnum, who offered US$50,000 to anyone who could provide the carcass of the lake creature.

While Barnum's prize was never claimed, over the decades several people have come forward with what they say is evidence of Champ's existence. In 1977, Sandra Mansi, a tourist from Connecticut, photo-graphed a large reptilian creature swimming in the waters of the lake. A 2005 video shot by fisherman Dick Affolter from his boat is said to capture Champ in motion, swimming just beneath the surface of the water.

It has been suggested that Champ may be a plesiosaur, a carnivorous aquatic reptile generally thought to have died out at the end of the Cretaceous period, well over 65 million years ago. Similar speculation has been made about Scotland's Loch Ness Monster, with proponents noting that both live in long, narrow, deep, cold bodies of water. It is, however, this very geographical feature that sceptics have latched on to as providing an

explanation for at least some of the sightings: bodies of water like Lake Champlain and Loch Ness are known to create seiches, underwater waves that raise debris from the bottom to the surface. Sceptics argue it is merely this debris that is seen, and not large creatures swimming in the waters.

Seiches have also been observed in British Columbia's Lake Okanagan, which is home to Ogopogo, Canada's most famous lake creature.

As with Champ, stories of Ogopogo are found in the legends of Canada's First Nations. Native tales tell of the creature inhabiting Rattlesnake Island, a small, barren piece of land located near the town of Peachland, a far more pleasant-sounding location on the southern half of the lake. In Salish culture, Ogopogo is known as 'N'ha-a-tik', which is translated variously as 'lake monster' or 'lake

**Bodies of water like Lake Champlain and Loch Ness are known to create seiches, underwater waves that raise debris from the bottom to the surface.**

demon'. The creature was said to be able to leave the water, often leaving the carcasses of its kills on the shore. In some accounts, when crossing the lake, small animals were thrown overboard by

ABOVE :
**The plesiosaur, considered by some to be the answer to the mysteries of Champ and the Loch Ness Monster.**

First Nations people in order to appease the monster. This custom was adopted by many early settlers to the area, with the apparent exception of one John MacDougall who, in the mid 1800s, is said to have lost a team of horses when they were simply sucked underwater by the monster.

For the Sushwap and Okanakane people, the *N'ha-a-tik* had supernatural power not only over the lake, but the wind as well. Indeed, one First Nations legend tells of the influence of the gods in creating *N'ha-a-tik*. In this story a man named Kel-Oni-Won murders an elder and is transformed into the lake monster as punishment. Unable to leave Lake Okanagan, he must spend eternity in the proximity of the scene of his horrible crime. He is shunned by all, except the rattlesnake.

There is an intriguing possibility that *N'ha-a-tik*, despite having been cursed to forever swim the lake, is dead. In 1914, a group of First Nations men came upon a decomposing carcass on the shore facing Rattlesnake Island. Described as being of a blue-grey colour, a little less than two metres (6 feet) long, the creature had a tail and flippers.

Assuming it really was *N'ha-a-tik* that was found rotting on the shores of Lake Okanagan, this would support the more recent argument made by many cryptozoologists that Ogopogo is, in fact, a different creature entirely.

Indeed, the first accounts of a mysterious zoological – as opposed to supernatural – being living in Lake Okanagan date from 1920, six years after the unidentified carcass was discovered. Since that time there have been over 200 sightings of Ogopogo.

Among the more notable is one captured by Ken Chaplain in 1989 on video. Another was reported by Daryl Ellis who, in 2000, swam the 135-kilometre (80-mile) length of the lake in order to raise money for cancer research. On 24 August of that year, he reported that for two hours a pair of Ogopogos had swum underneath him.

The lake monster is most often described as having either very dark green or very dark brown skin, but few if any scales. Its back is said to be particularly smooth, with a saw-toothed ridge running down the spine. There are, however, conflicting accounts regarding the creature's head – some likening it to that of a snake, while others have compared it variously to a sheep, horse, bulldog or alligator. Some witnesses report sparse hair, while others say that Ogopogo appears to have a mane. Occasionally, reports come through that claim the creature has ears or horns.

Those who have dismissed the numerous sightings of Ogopogo and Champ have theorized that they are simply the product of overactive imaginations; what witnesses actually saw were ducks, logs, or in the case of Ogopogo, seals swimming in a row. Sadly, it may take the exhibition of an actual lake monster carcass to settle the issue. The possibility of such an event is more likely in the case of Champ than it is for Ogopogo: to be to the safe side, in September 1989, the Government of British Columbia had Ogopogo listed as a protected species under their Wildlife Act.

## THE MYSTERY OF OGOPOGO'S NAME

Like Champ, Ogopogo's popular name has nothing to do with First Nations culture and legends. In fact, the origin of the silly-sounding moniker has been traced back no further than 1924, when Bill Brimblecomb, a man from the Okanagan Valley, sang at a Rotary Club luncheon in Vernon. The lyrics to Brimblecomb's song, said to have been written by H. F. Beattie, included the lines:

*I'm looking for the Ogopogo,*
*His mother was a mutton,*
*His father was a whale.*
*I'm going to put a little bit of salt on his tail.*

It seems a straightforward story. However, there is some debate as to the words Brimblecomb sang. The year 1924 also saw the publication of a British music hall song titled *The Ogo-Pogo: The Funny Fox-Trot*. Written by Cumberland Clark with music by Mark Strong, it contains the words:

*His mother was an earwig;*
*His father was a whale;*
*A little bit of head*
*And hardly any tail –*
*And Ogo-Pogo was his name.*

Might the song that Brimblecomb performed been Clark and Strong's? Like so much about Ogopogo, the answer remains a mystery.

# The Sasquatch Walks the Pacific Northwest

It was dubbed 'Bigfoot Friday' – 15 August 2008 – the day of a news conference held in Palo Alto, California, by charismatic promoter Tom Biscardi, CEO of Searching for Bigfoot Inc. At long last, the world would be presented with conclusive proof of the existence of the legendary ape-like creature, also known as the Sasquatch, which many believe inhabits the Pacific Northwest. Over 100 reporters covered the event; CNN carried the news conference live. It would appear that they had little concern with Biscardi's track record.

## Those who claim to have seen the Sasquatch describe the creature as having large eyes and a low-set forehead.

In July 2005, this Bigfoot enthusiast, then the CEO and Founder of the Great American Research Organization, had appeared on the late-night American radio show *Coast to Coast AM*, claiming near certainty that his organization would soon be successful in capturing the creature. He returned the following month to report that he was aware of a captured Sasquatch, and would provide footage of the animal over the internet to all willing to pay a $14 fee. However, when the day arrived on which the footage would be shown,

Biscardi announced that he had been deceived and that there was no specimen in captivity.

And yet, three years later, it appeared that all was forgotten. Over the course of the month, the American media had displayed precious little scepticism in following the story of a purported Sasquatch carcass. The frenzy – for it was a frenzy – grew out of YouTube postings in which Rick Dyer, a state trooper, and Matthew Whitton, a former correctional officer, claimed that an associate of theirs, identified only as a 'felon', had killed a Sasquatch. These initial statements, made in mid-June, were followed on 9 July by a posting in which it was revealed that the two men had retrieved the body. Dyer and Whitton were contacted by Biscardi and were given US$50,000 in cash for the frozen remains.

Those who attended the new conference of the self-proclaimed 'Real Bigfoot Hunter' were disappointed. Instead of the frozen Sasquatch carcass, reporters were presented with confusing and inconclusive DNA evidence, blurry photographs and a story of discovery that did not match those previously presented.

The following day the supposed Sasquatch carcass was thawed and found to be a commercially available rubber costume.

The sorry episode was another, perhaps the worst, in a series that sent shudders through the rather large and

diverse community of Sasquatch researchers. The media may have been duped, but the researchers had not; many had recognized the hoax well before Biscardi's involvement.

Stories of the Sasquatch pre-date the arrival of European explorers in North America. The creature is known by a number of names, a reflection of the continent's diverse indigenous population. Most share a common knowledge of a bipedal humanoid, usually between two and three metres (6 to 10 feet) in height, weighing in excess of 200 kilograms (450 lb), covered in reddish or brown hair. Typically, those who claim to have seen the Sasquatch describe the creature as having large eyes and a low-set forehead.

Casts of purported Sasquatch footprints invariably depict an enormous track – up to 60 centimetres (2 feet) in length and 20 centimetres

## A bulldozer operator claimed to have discovered enormous footprints while constructing a road in Bluff Creek Valley.

(8 inches) in width. The majority of tracks reported consist of five toes, though numbers between two and six have also been recorded.

Although the greatest concentration of Sasquatch sightings has been in the Pacific Northwest, a great number have been reported throughout the rest of North America, including all provinces and territories of Canada.

Native legends vary in the details of this large creature. Several indigenous cultures speak of a large hairy being with a basket that kidnaps children to eat. Others describe the 'kwi-kwiyai' or 'stiyaha' that carry off children who dare to say their names. In his 1859 travelogue, *Wanderings of an Artist Among the Indians of North America*, Paul Kane wrote of cannibalistic giants

living on the peak of Washington's Mount St Helens that the First Nations called 'skoocooms'.

It wasn't until the early 20th century, in a series of popular newspaper articles penned by Canadian J. W. Burns, that the various native legends of giants and hairy ape-like men were brought together. Though these stories varied in physical description and behaviour, Burns believed all concerned a single creature. A teacher on British Columbia's Chehalis Indian Reserve, Burns became the first to name this being the Sasquatch, a name he derived from the Salishan word 'sésquac', meaning 'wild man'.

In spite of Burns' articles, interest in the Sasquatch was, for the next few decades, limited to those with an interest in First Nations culture. It was not until the mid 20th century that the Sasquatch really began to take hold in non-native consciousness.

In 1958, a bulldozer operator named Gerold Crew claimed to have discovered enormous footprints, 40 centimetres (15 inches) in length, while constructing a road in Bluff Creek Valley, a remote area of Humboldt County, California. Plaster casts were made and the finding was duly reported in the local newspaper under the title 'Bigfoot'. The story was then picked up by the Associated Press, and thus another name for the creature was coined.

It wasn't long before hunters descended on the valley, hoping to capture or kill the creature. While the Sasquatch has been seemingly elusive, the half-century that followed Crew's find has featured reports of sightings from across the United States. The vast majority have come from the Pacific Coast, though Texas, Ohio and Florida also appear to be favoured by the creature.

By far the most famous of all these sightings is recorded on the so-called Patterson-Gimlin film, shot in the same Bluff Creek Valley, by Roger Patterson and Robert Gimlin. Claimed by the

LEFT:
**A still from the 1967 Patterson-Gimlin film shot in Bluff Creek Valley, California.**

filmmakers as genuine footage of a Sasquatch, it depicts a tall, hairy bipedal creature covered in short black hair. Since its first showing, in the autumn of 1967, the Patterson-Gimlin film has been the matter of some debate within the scientific community. While some have dismissed the film outright as depicting a man in an ape suit, others have been more cautious. Among those arguing in support of the film was the late anthropologist Grover Krantz of Washington State University. In his awkwardly titled book, *Bigfoot Sasquatch: Evidence* he provides a detailed analysis of the creature's stride, and concludes that the movements could not have been made by a human. As such, he argues, we must concede that the creature depicted is unknown.

However, Krantz did speculate that the creature might be a relic form of gigantopithecus, an ape that roamed the regions of China, India and Vietnam, before dying out some 300,000 years ago. The theory is supported by the fact that the Bering land bridge, which once connected North America to Asia, was used as a migratory route by a great number of species. Those arguing against the gigantopithecus note that no fossils have been uncovered in North America. There is also debate within the scientific community as to whether the ape was bipedal or quadrupedal.

Whether a gigantopithecus or a previously unknown animal, it would seem that the Sasquatch population is not in a healthy state. Before his death in 2002, Krantz estimated there were approximately only 2,000 Sasquatches roaming the huge wilderness areas of British Columbia, Washington, Oregon and northern California.

Much of the evidence cited by those arguing the existence of the Sasquatch involves plaster casts and photographs of footprints. Here, again, there has been considerable debate concerning authenticity. While acknowledging that there had been hoaxes, Krantz argued that elements such as spacing between

prints and pressure ridges, small mounds of soil produced by the forefoot prior to leaving the ground, could not be faked.

Amongst his colleagues, Krantz was very much a voice of the minority.

ABOVE:
**The late anthropologist Grover Krantz holding a plaster cast of a Sasquatch footprint.**

Within the scientific and academic communities, talk of the Sasquatch is met with great scepticism, primarily due to a curious lack of physical evidence. Despite decades of dedication on behalf of Sasquatch believers, no specimen has been caught, no remains have been discovered and no fossil records have been found. In 2000, the body cast of what is purported to be a Sasquatch's behind, ankles, thigh, hip and left arm collected by the Bigfoot

Field Researchers Organization was dismissed as being the imprint of an elk (indeed, hairs identified as being from elk and bear have been found in the cast).

Sceptics observe that North America, particularly those regions said to be favoured by the creature, offers a particularly inhospitable environment for a nonhuman primate. Moreover, if the Sasquatch does exist, it would need to be a migratory creature.

In winter, the forests of the Pacific Northwest do not produce the abundance of vegetation that a large primate would require to live. Like the black bear, it would certainly be tempted by garbage placed outside suburban homes on the edge of cities, yet no such sightings have yet been reported.

## SASQUATCH MURDERS

The Sasquatch is invariably described as a threatening creature. It is therefore not surprising that the creature is considered to be capable of murdering a human. While such stories are a staple of supermarket tabloids, a number of serious works on the Sasquatch do cover the topic. Some speculate that *The Wilderness Hunter*, a book written by Theodore Roosevelt before he assumed the presidency of the United States, may contain an account of a murder by a Sasquatch. The passages in question relate to a tale passed on by an old mountain hunter identified only as 'Bauman'. In the man's youth, so the story goes, he was trapping with another man when their camp was twice ransacked. Though they had not been present on either occasion, some sign of who might be to blame was provided by some very large footprints. One evening Bauman was awoken by a sound and was struck immediately by 'a strong, wild-beast odor'. Through the darkness he spotted a 'great body', which ran off after the trapper fired his gun. Eventually, the two men decided to leave the area. As they collected their traps, both men experienced the unpleasant sensation that they were being followed. Bauman separated from his companion to gather the final three traps and returned to camp to find the unnamed man lying dead with a broken neck. After seeing teeth marks on the victim's throat, Bauman abandoned the camp, fleeing with nothing but his rifle. According to Roosevelt, the elderly hunter believed that the creature he'd encountered had been something 'half human or half devil, some great goblin-beast'.

The only other report of anyone having been killed at the rather large hands of a Sasquatch is that of a man variously named John Mire or John McGuire, in 1943. His supposed murder is mentioned, with surprisingly little fanfare, in a number of books on the creature. Brief and vague accounts of the event, depict Mire – or McGuire – as having been attacked by a Sasquatch, before his dogs drove the beast away. He subsequently died of his injuries. A few sources go so far as to quote his headstone: 'John McGuire, 1901–1943 Killed by Bigfoot'. The exact location of the victim's grave has not been reported, and it should be noted that the term 'Bigfoot' wasn't coined until 1958, 15 years after the supposed murder. The story of the Mire/McGuire murder is generally discounted by Sasquatch enthusiasts.

# The Flesh-Hungry Wendigo

On 15 June 1907, at Caribou Lake, Manitoba, the Royal North-West Mounted Police (RNWMP) arrested two men on a charge of murder. Jack Fiddler and his brother Joseph were both members of the Sucker people at Sandy Lake. Indeed, the group viewed Jack, whose true name was Zhauwuno-geezhigo-gaubow ('He who stands in the southern sky') as its leader.

The Sucker people lived in a remote area of the province, and spoke an uncommon form of the Oji-Cree language. Concentrated almost entirely on relations with their allies the Pelican and Sturgeon clans, relations with other people were extremely limited. It wasn't until 1899 that the first missionary visited Sandy Lake, and even then he stayed no more than two days.

Jack Fiddler's leadership of his group was supported by his acknowledged powers as a shaman, the greatest of which was his ability to defeat the lethal Wendigo.

While descriptions of the Wendigo vary, it is commonly depicted as a wicked, disruptive creature, possessing supernatural abilities. Of all the creatures found in First Nations culture, the Wendigo appears as the most terrifying, both in actions and appearance. It most frequently appears during the winter months, or during times of great famine and starvation. An emaciated cannibal, the creature is described as having large, bulging eyes that swim in blood. Its hands are big, with long fingers and claw-like fingernails while its feet are said to be almost a metre (3 feet) in length and feature a single toe. As it has a heart of ice, the evil being is insensitive to cold.

Wendigos apparently fall on their prey without warning. Using their sharp, jagged teeth, they rip the flesh with a ferocity manifested by greed. Growing larger with each person consumed, the creature cannot ever be satisfied, and must always turn its attention to the next

ABOVE:
In recent years, the Wendigo has re-entered popular culture, including depictions in comic books.

victim. No amount of eating, it seems, can put flesh on a Wendigo's bones.

According to legend, a person might be transformed into a Wendigo, either after having resorted to cannibalism, or through simple possession.

There have been several documented cases in which individuals, fearing that they were becoming the creature, have asked to be executed. In extreme cases, these requests were carried out, usually after attempts to heal through traditional means had failed.

Jack Fiddler had killed fourteen Wendigos in his lifetime. A number were said to have been sent against his people by enemy shamans, while others were members of the Sucker people who had either become or were in danger of becoming Wendigos.

Despite the limited contact of the Sucker people with others outside their group, Jack Fiddler's reputation as a

strong shaman had spread throughout the area. His arrest had occurred after stories that the Sucker folk were 'in the habit of killing one another whenever one gets delirious through fever or other causes' had reached the Mounted Police. During their investigation, they learned that Jack Fiddler and his brother Joseph (also known as Pesequan) had killed a woman – who was said to be in danger of becoming a Wendigo – in the autumn of 1905. Wahsakapeequay, the deceased, was Joseph's daughter-in-law.

Not everyone believed that the brothers should have been arrested. Gilbert Edward Sanders, Superintendent of the RNWMP, was irritated by the charges, and suggested that they be dropped. He was particularly concerned over Jack Fiddler's health. Although nothing could be said with any certainty, it was estimated that the leader of the Sucker people was somewhere in the

ABOVE:
**At the trial of Jack Fiddler, it was reported that a delirious Wahsakapeequay had been restrained by several women.**

area of 75 years of age. Methodist missionary Joseph Albert George Lousley also suggested that the arrest had been a mistake, describing Jack Fiddler as 'a quiet dignified man who has lived his life with a clear conscience'.

However, the prosecution proceeded with its case. On 30 September, while still awaiting trial, Jack Fiddler managed to slip away from his guard and walk into the bush. He was found dead later in the day, having used a sash to hang himself from a tree.

## She sat cross-legged with her head wrapped in a shawl, as Charlebois struck her skull with a club.

Seven days later, the case against Joseph Fiddler was presented before a jury. He had no lawyer, nor were any witnesses called in his defence. The prosecution's case rested on the testimony of Minowapawin, the husband of one of the Sucker people. He reported that in the hours leading up to her death he had twice seen Wahsakapeequay. She had become extremely ill and violent; it had taken several women to hold her down. When he looked in on her the following day, Wahsakapeequay was being cared for by Jack and Joseph Fiddler. According to Minowapawin, the ill woman lay quietly as the two men placed a string around her neck and strangled her.

The witness also spoke of three other Wendigo killings that had taken place amongst the Sucker people, thus introducing evidence that was prejudicial to the case.

Nevertheless, the six-man jury recommended mercy, despite returning a guilty verdict. There would be none. Aylesworth Bowen Perry, the stipendiary magistrate, sentenced Joseph Fiddler to hang – just as his brother had.

However, the sentence handed down by Perry would not be carried out.

Numerous people, including three of the jurors, fought on behalf of Joseph Fiddler, and there was a concerted letter-writing campaign to save his life. Fiddler could do little himself. He spent nearly all of his incarceration at Stony Mountain Penitentiary in the prison infirmary.

His sentence was soon commuted to life in prison and, on 4 September 1909, after an effort of nearly two years, the once-condemned man was ordered to be released. It was too late. Three days earlier, Joseph Fiddler – Pesequan – had died of consumption.

The trial of Joseph Fiddler was the last in a small number of Wendigo-related cases to come before the courts. Another, similar to the Fiddler case as its occurrence was due to tribal beliefs and practices, took place at Battleford, Northwest Territories, on 27 November 1885, shortly after the North-West Rebellion. The defendants, Charlebois, Bright Eyes and Dressy Man, were charged with the murder of an elderly woman named She Wills, all members of Big Bear's Cree band.

The purported murder took place on 13 April 1885, after the victim announced that she would soon become a Wendigo. It was She Wills' request that someone kill her. Charlebois, Bright Eyes and Dressy Man were chosen to carry out the task due, at least in part, to their experience as warriors. The elderly woman was carried from the band's encampment and placed on the ground. There, she sat cross-legged with her head wrapped in a shawl, as Charlebois struck her skull with a club. Bright Eyes then shot her three times, after which Dressy Man used a sabre to behead her. He made a point of throwing her head in the brush, well away from the body. The three warriors then ran back to camp, fearing the spirits they had unleashed. She Wills' body was buried the next day as a means of preventing its reuniting with the head.

All was done in accordance with ritual so that the Wendigo would not be able to use She Wills' body to feed upon band members.

The jury hearing the case delivered a mixed verdict: Charlebois and Dressy Man were convicted of murder, while Bright Eyes was found guilty of manslaughter. Bright Eyes received a sentence of twenty years. Though Charlebois and Dressy Man were sentenced to hang, this was later commuted to life in prison.

Of all the trials related to the Wendigo, that of Swift Runner stands alone. This Plains Cree trapper did not kill the cannibalistic creature; he became one.

Those who knew him recognized that Swift Runner had a strong connection with the spirit world. He had for many years encountered the Wendigo, reporting to others that the creature had been encouraging him to become a cannibal.

In the autumn of 1878, Swift Runner, his wife and seven children left their home, some one hundred kilometres (60 miles) north of what was then known as Fort Edmonton, for new trapping grounds on the west bank of Sturgeon Creek. He returned home in the spring, claiming that his family had starved to death during what had been a particularly cold winter. What clouded this story was the fact that the teller appeared to have suffered no malnourishment. When he failed to provide an adequate explanation for their absence, his wife's family alerted the Mounted Police. A subsequent patrol mounted to Swift Runner's new trapping grounds uncovered evidence of cannibalism, and he was arrested.

At his trial, held 8 August 1879 in Fort Edmonton, Swift Runner was quick to confess the murders. He explained that the killing had started after he'd been hunting and had returned to camp unable to get the cries of the trapped animals out of his head. Swift Runner was sentenced to hang, the very punishment that he wished to carry out himself. He had to be placed on suicide watch until the day of his execution.

Swift Runner's story, the only documented case of a person who thought he had been possessed by a Wendigo, is often cited by modern scholars who argue that the cannibalistic being may be explained by a psychosis. It is pointed out that Swift Runner did not have to resort to cannibalism, as his trapping grounds were a mere 30 kilometres (18 miles) away from the nearest Hudson's Bay Company post. Swift Runner appeared to be well aware of this fact – but even if he hadn't been, how does one explain that he felt the need to kill and consume each and every member of his family?

## Just as the Wendigo seems to have disappeared from existence, the creature has been used with increasing frequency in horror movies and novels.

Scholars seeking to account for acts such as these have applied the term: 'Wendigo psychosis', described by anthropologist Robert A. Brightman as 'an Algonquian-specific psychiatric disorder whose sufferers experienced and acted upon obsessional cannibalistic urges.'

Cases of Wendigo psychosis, once rare, are now considered unheard of. However, just as the Wendigo seems to have disappeared from existence, the creature has been used with increasing frequency in horror movies and novels. The earliest appearance of the creature in a work of fiction came from the pen of English writer Algernon Blackwood. His horror story 'The Wendigo' was inspired by a 1898 visit to the Ontario city of Kenora, which was then known by the less appealing name of Rat Portage. The region surrounding Lake of the Woods, in which Kenora is situated, was once thought to have the highest concentration of Wendigos, and has been described as the 'Wendigo capital of the world'.

## TERROR AMONG THE TRAPPERS

RIGHT:
A Hudson's Bay
Company post, where
traders also lived in
fear of the mysterious
Wendigo.

Fear of the Wendigo was not limited to the Algonquian-speaking tribes, but spread to those with whom they came into contact. In the late 18th century, explorer David Thompson wrote about the creature, as did Sir William Francis Butler in his 1872 work *The Great Lone Land*. **George Bryce's** *The Remarkable History of the Hudson's Bay Company,* written in 1900, provides perhaps the best record of the extent to which belief in the Wendigo affected those working in the fur trade:

The story of the Wendigo was an alarming one. No crew would push on after the sun was set, lest they should see this apparition.

Some said he was a spirit condemned to wander the earth on account of crimes committed, while others believed the Wendigo was a desperate outcast who had tasted human flesh and prowled about at night in the camping-places of traders searching for victims. Tales were told of unlucky trappers who had disappeared in the woods and had never been heard of again. The story of the Wendigo made the camping-place to be surrounded [sic] with a sombre interest to the traders.

Unbelievers in this mysterious ogre freely declared that it was but a partner's story told to prevent the voyageurs delaying on their journey, and to hinder them from wandering to lonely spots by the rapids to fish or hunt. One of the old writers spoke of the enemy of the voyageurs —

*'Il se nourrit des corps des pauvres voyageurs, Des malheureux passants et des navigateurs.'*
('He feeds on the bodies of unfortunate men of the river, of unlucky travellers, and of the mariners.')

# CHAPTER 2:
# HISTORICAL UNKNOWNS

# Leif the Lucky and the Yarmouth Stone

Nova Scotia's Yarmouth County Museum houses a large 200-kilogram (440-pound) stone. By far the most famous and most popular artefact on display, at first glance it appears no different from any other stone that might be found in the grounds outside the museum's walls. However, closer inspection reveals thirteen clearly cut markings – proof, say believers, that Vikings once sailed the waters of Yarmouth Harbour.

Doctor Richard Fletcher, a retired army surgeon, claimed to have stumbled over the stone in 1812, in a cove not far from the harbour's head. After the discovery, it was transported closer to the Fletcher home, where it remained for some six decades, visible to passers-by and anyone who cared to look out of the dining room window.

As the years passed the value of the Yarmouth Stone as an attraction was recognized, and in 1872 it was moved to the grounds of a local hotel. Not to be outdone, a competing establishment later began displaying its own artefact, known as the Bay View Stone, which featured a similar-looking inscription. This second stone, since lost, was the creation of the hotel owner, and was used as a means of attracting business. Eventually, the Yarmouth Stone was given to the Yarmouth Public Library, which has since loaned it to the museum.

Is the stone evidence of Viking exploration in and around Yarmouth?

The first body to make such a claim was the Numismatic and Antiquarian Society of Philadelphia, which identified the markings as the work of Norsemen.

In his 1884 book *On a Supposed Runic Inscription at Yarmouth, Nova Scotia*, Henry Phillips, Jr, a scholar known for his translations from German and Spanish, wrote that the stone read either: 'Harkko spoke to his men' or 'Harkko's son spoke to the men'. Those who hold this interpretation as correct believe that Harkko is in actuality Haki, a companion of Karlsefni, found in Norse sagas.

The most sensational translation belongs to Olaf Strandwold, a Norwegian scholar and County Superintendent of Schools in Benton County, Washington. In 1934, Strandwold published a 16-page booklet, *The Yarmouth Stone: Mystic Characters on Yarmouth Stone Yield Startling Evidence of Norse Discoveries*, in which he claimed that the markings found on the

BELOW:
**A depiction of the settlement founded by Leif Eriksson at L'Anse aux Meadows.**

LEFT:
The Knights Templar, one of the groups credited with the mysterious inscription on the Yarmouth Stone.

Yarmouth Stone read 'Leif to Eric raises'. The object being raised, argued the translator, is the stone itself. According to Strandwold and those who hold his translation to be true, 'Leif' is Leif Eriksson, the first European to set foot in the New World and son of Erik the Red, the recipient of the tribute. Thus, the Yarmouth Stone was presented as evidence that Leif Eriksson, also known as Leif the Lucky, once sailed into Yarmouth Harbour.

Others have claimed that the markings are the work of the Knights Templar or Freemasons, or is in some way related to the as-yet uncovered Oak Island Money Pit. At one time or another the inscription has been claimed to be old Japanese, ancient Basque, Greek and Hungarian.

Study of the stone has been made difficult as its original markings have been defaced through misguided efforts to make them more legible. Indeed, a mid 18th-century description of the Yarmouth Stone records that the inscription: 'barely penetrated the quartz'. At some point, perhaps when it was being used as a lure for hotel guests, white paint was applied to the markings. In the 1930s, in another attempt to make the inscription more legible, the Reverend Gordon T. Lewis, first President of the Yarmouth

Historical Society, decided to re-chisel the stone.

The reverend was a great believer in the stone and argued with unwavering certainty that Vikings had explored great stretches of North America. Much of his opinion is found in *The Cruise of the Knorr*, a self-published pamphlet covering Leif the Lucky's visit to Yarmouth, as evidenced by the Yarmouth Stone, and a rather romantic discussion of 'Leif's Great House', which supposedly once overlooked the Tusket River in Yarmouth County.

## The Yarmouth Stone was presented as evidence that Leif Eriksson, also known as Leif the Lucky, once sailed into Yarmouth Harbour.

Some scholars have argued that the markings aren't European in origin, but are the work of the Mi'kmaq. In her 1973 book, *Rock Drawings of the Micmac Indians*, Marion Robertson notes a similarity between the marks cut into the stone and petroglyphs found in rocks at other locations in Nova Scotia.

Whether the Yarmouth Stone is a hoax continues to be a matter of debate. However, in Yarmouth itself there are few believers. Among the sceptics are Richard Fletcher's descendants, who have argued that the good doctor put his considerable surgical skills to use in carving the stone. An intelligent, highly educated man, Fletcher was known to have had a mischievous nature and a unique sense of humour.

Most archaeologists place the Yarmouth Stone with Minnesota's Kensington Runestone – another stone with rune marks found in 1898 – and dismiss both as hoaxes. It has been pointed out that the two stones came to light during periods when people were eager to find evidence of Norse exploration in North America outside Greenland.

The wait for conclusive proof was a long one. It wasn't until 1960, nearly 150 years after Fletcher's supposed discovery of the Yarmouth Stone, that remnants of a Norse settlement were famously uncovered at L'Anse aux Meadows, in the province of Newfoundland and Labrador. Dating back approximately 1,000 years, the site has the remains of eight buildings and numerous artefacts, including a whetstone, a bone knitting needle, a stone oil lamp and a bronze fastening pin.

Tellingly, however, archaeologists uncovered no inscribed stone monuments.

RIGHT:
A reconstruction of the ancient Norse settlement at L'Anse aux Meadows, Newfoundland.

# THE LAND OF WINE

Within years of establishing their first settlement in Greenland, Vikings under Leif Eriksson began to explore three lands even further west. The first, Helluland – 'land of flat stones' – we know as Baffin Island; the second, Markland – 'land of forests' or 'land of wood' – is generally accepted as being part of the Labrador shore. The third, however, has been the subject of much debate and speculation. Known as Vinland – usually thought to mean 'land of wine' – it was considered the most amenable of all North American land explored by the Vikings. Over 1,000 years later, the question remains, where is Vinland? Certainly this land of wine could not be L'Anse aux Meadows, a location that even in this time of global warming is not suitable for growing grapes. Various locations, invariably further south, have been claimed as the true location of Vinland, including Anticosti Island, the Gaspé Peninsula, Cape Breton Island, the mainland of Nova Scotia, the northeast coast of New Brunswick, Massachusetts and Rhode Island.

Some have argued that the name Vinland is nothing more than a marketing ploy, used by Leif Eriksson and Erik the Red to encourage others to follow. After all, the latter had given the name Greenland to an island covered almost entirely by ice and snow.

Another possibility is that the wine made in this 'land of wine' was derived from blueberries and gooseberries. Both grow in abundance on the Island of Newfoundland and are suitable for making wine.

The answer to the mystery of Vinland may be provided by modern scholarship. In recent years it has been proposed that Leif Eriksson's name for the land he visited referred, in fact, to the lush grass that grew there, which would have been so crucial to their keeping livestock. Despite the neat link this provides with its modern name, it has been suggested that L'Anse aux Meadows could be an anglicized corruption of L'Anse aux Meduse (Jellyfish Cove), from the French fishermen working there during the 16th through 19th centuries.

ABOVE LEFT:
The Vikings pushed their exploration west of Greenland to Baffin Island.

MIDDLE:
Labrador shore, known to the Vikings as the 'land of forests'.

BOTTOM:
The location of the mysterious Vinland remains unknown to this day.

# William Shakespeare, Marie Antoinette and the Money Pit

Canada has more islands than any other nation, and some of the very largest. From the Arctic islands that defeated the Franklin Expedition to the island colonies of occultist Brother XII, they have served as the locations of the country's greatest mysteries. For treasure hunters, however, one island stands alone. A 57-hectare (140-acre) body of land off the coast of Nova Scotia, one of roughly 350 islands in Mahone Bay, Oak Island has been said to hold variously great treasures of pirates, literature, the French monarchy and Christianity.

The mystery of Oak Island stretches back to 1795, when 16-year-old Daniel McGinnis came upon a circular depression adjacent to a tree with a tackle block on an overhanging branch.

With the help of friends McGinnis began excavating and uncovered a layer of flagstones a few feet below the surface of the depression. This was followed by several log coverings. After digging down some 10 metres (30 feet), McGinnis and his friends gave up on the excavation.

In the early years of the 19th century, a group known as the Onslow Company continued the excavation to a depth of roughly 27 metres (90 feet). In doing so, they brought to the surface putty and charcoal. The best news for the treasure seekers lay in their discovery of coconut fibres, which was once used in shipping to protect valuable objects. It would seem that the Onslow Company had arrived at Oak Island convinced that treasure lay beneath. If so, they

LEFT:
The legendary pirate Captain Kidd, one of the historical figures whose treasure is said to be buried on the island.

FAR LEFT:
Just a few of the buildings constructed during two centuries of digging the Money Pit.

must have been even more heartened when they uncovered a large stone bearing an inscription in code. The symbols it featured have been translated several times; the most accepted version reading: 'Forty feet below, two million pounds lie buried.'

If this story is at all accurate, the men of the Onslow Company must have looked on in horror when, on returning to the pit for another day's work one morning, they discovered it filled with water to a level of 10 metres (30 feet). When bailing proved ineffective, the Company gave up all hope of retrieving the treasure and left the island.

In 1849, investors in an organization called the Truro Company managed to excavate the pit to 26 metres (85 feet) before it again flooded. They attempted to deal with the water by drilling below the bottom of the pit, apparently hitting spruce, oak and unidentified metal before abandoning the project.

The history of the excavation becomes clearer after 1856, when reports began appearing in the *Liverpool Transcript*. At this point, what had come to be called the Money Pit was considered to be the place of great treasure hidden by the 17th-century Scottish pirate William 'Captain' Kidd.

In 1861, a company known as the Oak Island Association began a three-year search for the treasure. The venture is perhaps best remembered for the first of the six fatalities associated with the excavations, which occurred when a boiler burst. Ultimately, the Oak Island Association was thwarted by the collapse of the bottom of the pit and a subsequent lack of funds.

The promise of great treasure prompted numerous other excavations, and attracted plenty of investors. Franklin D. Roosevelt is just one of the hundreds of people who have sunk their money into the pit. Gilbert Hedden, the wealthy Vice-President of the Hedden Iron Construction Company, was so convinced that the Money Pit held Captain Kidd's treasure that he purchased the southeast end of the island. In 1939, four years into his excavations, he made a point of reporting his progress to King George VI.

In the 1960s, a causeway was constructed so that a 70-ton digging crane could be brought on to the island. Employing a clam bucket, it dug into the pit to a depth of 40 metres (130 feet), and expanded the width to 30 metres (100 feet). As the decade drew to a

## A closed-circuit monitor is said to have shown the outlines of three chests, a pickaxe, a severed hand and a corpse.

close, yet another concern, Triton Alliance Ltd, bought most of Oak Island. They claimed to have excavated a 72-metre (235-foot) shaft, supported by a steel caisson, into which they lowered a remote-controlled under-water camera. A closed-circuit monitor is said to have shown the outlines of three chests, a pickaxe, a severed hand and a corpse. The shaft subsequently collapsed, and there has been little to no excavation at the site since the late 1980s.

Some have claimed that the circular depression that young Daniel McGinnis stumbled upon over two centuries ago was nothing more than a natural phenomenon, most likely a sinkhole with natural caverns beneath it. The 60-year period between the discovery and the reports of the Money Pit is viewed with suspicion. Moreover, there are no surviving materials from the flagstones and log platforms that were said to have been uncovered during the early excavations. No one knows the location of the block that McGinnis is said to have seen above the hole. Indeed, there is no evidence to suggest that the tree to which the block was attached even existed.

To sceptics, the flooding that has occurred with nearly every excavation has nothing to do with man-made tunnels and booby-traps, as has been asserted, but is simply explained by underground streams. Indeed, numerous sinkholes, underground streams and subterranean caves are known to exist on the mainland, very close to Oak Island.

It has been argued that man-made structures found at the site, such as oak planks, are merely remnants of previous excavation attempts.

Finally, sceptics point to the large inscribed stone supposedly found in the early 19th century. This stone, of which no photographs, rubbings or other images exist, is said to have been lost in the early 20th century. Despite the stone's significance, no mention was made of its existence until 1951 – long after its disappearance – when historian Edward Rowe Snow described it in his book *True Tales of Buried Treasure*. A specialist in the study of pirates, Snow said that he was given the symbols by a Reverend A. T. Kempton of Cambridge, Massachusetts. There is no record that the reverend, a sometime lecturer on Longfellow, was ever involved in the Oak Island excavations.

However, there are those who maintain that Oak Island holds great secrets. Speculation as to the purpose behind the pit is remarkably varied.

The earliest recorded belief, as featured in the *Liverpool Transcript*, supposes that the Money Pit contains the treasure of Captain Kidd. A related theory holds that it is another pirate – Edward Teach, better known as Blackbeard – who buried his treasure on Oak Island.

There has been some speculation that the treasure thought to be beneath the surface of the island has nothing to do with pirates; rather, that the elaborate Money Pit was constructed by shipwrecked Spanish sailors who looked to hide the riches that their wrecked galleon had been carrying.

War rears its ugly head in other theories. If correct, the pit was either built by the French, who sought to hide the treasure of Louisbourg from the English, or it was constructed by the

## Numerous sinkholes, underground streams and subterranean caves are known to exist on the mainland, very close to Oak Island.

English, who wanted to keep funds from the Americans during the Revolutionary War.

Though each suggestion has elements of danger and excitement, they lack documentation. A more romantic

BELOW: Blackbeard, the 18th-century pirate who sailed the Caribbean Sea and western Atlantic.

ABOVE:
Marie Antoinette, the French queen who lost her life during the Reign of Terror.

Nova Scotia mainland to Great Britain. It seems rather unlikely that the French Navy would travel across the Atlantic to bury the jewels on British territory. If true, this would place the construction of the Money Pit within just a few years, or even less, of Daniel McGinnis' discovery.

One theory argues that the lost stone inscription was the writing of the Coptic Christians, early believers of Egyptian descent. That translation reads: 'The people shall not forget the Lord. To offset the hardships of winter and the onset of plague… the Arif, he shall pray to the Lord.' Those who hold this belief point out that Harry Marshall, the man who apparently brought the stone out of the shaft, thought its makeup unlike any of the stone he had encountered on the island. This, say proponents, is evidence that the stone was from Egypt, and that the treasure might very well be riches of the pharaohs.

A favourite theory amongst those with an interest in literature and the theatre was proposed by Penn Leary in his 1953 book, *The Oak Island Enigma: A History and Inquiry Into the Origin of the Money Pit*. Here, Leary claims that the English philosopher and statesman Francis Bacon had the Money Pit constructed in order to hide documents that proved himself the true author of William Shakespeare's works.

The enormous success of Dan Brown's 2003 novel *The Da Vinci Code* has reignited interest in a theory that holds Oak Island as the resting place of the Holy Grail. The premise relies almost exclusively on imagination, rather than documentation, beginning with the acceptance that the Knights Templar succeeded in finding the Grail some 800 years ago. Proponents argue that only the Templars would have had the knowledge to construct so sophisticated a resting place. If this theory holds true, those digging at Oak Island may very well one day uncover the greatest archaeological find in history.

theory, also without any archival support, proposes that the jewels of Marie Antoinette are buried in the Money Pit. Those supporting this theory point out that, save a few specimens, the jewels of the last queen of France are indeed missing. According to this premise, when the Palace of

## One romantic theory proposes that the jewels of Marie Antoinette are buried in the Money Pit.

Versailles was stormed in 1789, Marie Antoinette had a maid or a lady-in-waiting flee with the jewels. The woman eventually ended up on the other side of the Atlantic, on a little island off the coast of what is now Nova Scotia, where the French Navy constructed a pit in which to hide the jewels. It is a strange theory, one that ignores history; nearly eight decades earlier, France lost the

# THE CURSED LOST LEMON MINE

It is thought that buried treasure of a different sort may be found somewhere in Alberta's Crowsnest Pass. According to legend, in 1870 two American prospectors, Frank Lemon and a man known only as Blackjack, crossed into what was then the Northwest Territories from Montana, and began looking for gold in the foothills of Alberta. Before long, the two found more than they'd dared hope for beneath the bedrock of a small mountain stream.

That evening, after arguing as to how they might proceed, Lemon took an axe and killed Blackjack. Consumed with guilt, he went insane, and fled back to Montana. The next spring the crazed man led a team of prospectors to the Alberta foothills, but could not find the mine. He spent his final years at his brother's ranch in Texas, where he died, taking the secret with him.

One variation of the story tells that the axe murder was witnessed by some Blackfoot, who reported the crime to their chief, Jacob Bearspaw. A curse was then placed on the land so that it would not be taken over by the white man.

In support of the belief that the lost Lemon mine is cursed are stories of prospectors who after having found the mine, drink themselves to death or are consumed in house fires. In each case, they take the location of the gold to their grave.

Accounts of the lost Lemon mine are generally discounted by historians. Bearspaw is known to have made money from acting as a guide to prospectors in search of the mine. However, many have hoped to find elements of truth within the story.

While geologists have also dismissed stories of the riches held at Crowsnest Pass, one of their number, Ron Stewart, once claimed to have found the elusive mine. In 1989, his company, Crowsnest Metallics, put in a claim on a stretch of land outside Coleman. Ultimately, the mine was a failure, never yielding more than 2 grams (0.074 ounces) of gold per ton of rock.

The late historian Grant McEwan believed that the lost Lemon mine is nothing more than a great piece of Alberta folklore.

BLACKFOOT INDIANER ZU PFERD. | INDIEN PIEDS NOIR A CHEVAL.

LEFT:
Members of the Blackfoot Confederacy are said to have witnessed Blackjack's murder.

# The Massacre of the Donnellys

**The original Donnelly grave marker. Three metres (10 feet) in height, it was erected in 1889 by William Donnelly. It was replaced 75 years later.**

On 1 July 1879, the people of Canada marked the 12th anniversary of Confederation. Celebrations were invariably simple affairs – modest and quiet – very much a reflection of the young country. Just over four million Canadians were living in the Dominion's seven provinces and territories. In sharp contrast with the republic to the south, Canada boasted a low murder rate – it was said that in any given year the number of homicides could be counted on the hands of two or three men.

**In what was then described as 'the blackest crime ever committed in the Dominion', five people were murdered and a family home was burned to the ground.**

There were, however, areas of this largely rural country that were something less than placid. Lucan in Ontario's Biddulph Township, 25 kilometres (15 miles) north of London, is just one example. Once known as 'the wildest town in Canada', in the winter that followed the aforementioned celebration it became the focal point of a most shocking and brutal incident of vigilantism. In what was then described as 'the blackest crime ever committed in the Dominion', five people were murdered and a family home was burned to the ground. The brutal crimes and subsequent trial would leave a deep stain on Biddulph Township that endures to this day.

James Donnelly, the patriarch of the massacred family, was an Irish immigrant from County Tipperary, and is thought to have arrived in Canada in or around 1842. It can be said with greater certainty that by the spring of 1847, Donnelly was squatting in Biddulph Township in what was then known as Canada West. It is not known whether Donnelly was aware that he was living on land owned by another – an absentee landlord named James Grace who had purchased the lot from the Canada Company. Regardless, he was then a man of very limited means, and would have lacked the funds to purchase the land.

James Donnelly and his family had been living on the lot for a little less than a decade, clearing the land and farming, when it was sold to Patrick Farrell, another immigrant from Ireland. When the new owner arrived in Canada West, prepared to take possession, he was surprised to find the Donnelly family living on his land. A dispute ensued and it was a matter of a few months before Farrell and Donnelly faced each other in court. Though the new owner wanted the squatter evicted from his land, with great reluctance he reached an agreement in which Donnelly was permitted to keep 25 acres (10 hectares).

However, Farrell remained bitter over the concession he'd made and with great frequency spoke out in public against the Donnelly family. On 27 June 1857, the bad blood between the two men broke out in violence.

It all took place during the most unlikely of events: a barn raising, typically a time when a community comes together to help out one of its own. The two enemies began a drunken brawl, during which Donnelly threw an iron lever at Farrell's head. Two days later, the injured man died. When the authorities arrived to arrest Donnelly, the former squatter turned legitimate landowner was nowhere to be found. His wife, Johannah, refused to assist in the effort to find the wanted man.

Nearly two years passed before Donnelly resurfaced, turning himself in to the local Justice of the Peace. As it turned out, the fugitive had always been close at hand. James Donnelly had been living in his barn and had donned his wife's clothing as a disguise when working his fields.

On 17 September 1859, after a brief trial, the 43-year-old Donnelly was sentenced to hang. Johannah once again came to his aid, starting a petition for clemency that saw her husband's sentence reduced to a stretch of seven years served in Kingston Penitentiary.

During his incarceration, his family of wife and eight children managed to stay in Biddulph Township, working the land he'd laboured so hard to clear. In 1865, he returned to a more prosperous farm than the one he had left.

However, the troubles were not left in the past. The seven Donnelly sons, now growing into manhood, had several run-ins with the law. In 1869, William Donnelly, the second eldest, was charged with larceny. Shortly after he was acquitted, he was again before the court, this time accused of having robbed the Granton post office with his brother James Donnelly, Jr. Both were found innocent.

The next few years were active ones as the seven sons began struggling to make their ways in the world. In the spring of 1873, William founded the Donnelly Stagecoach Line, running between London, Exeter and Lucan. Operating with his brothers John, Michael and Thomas, the venture was a success from the start, and provided stiff competition for the Hawkshaw's Omnibus Line that had long operated in the area. That autumn, its owner, John Hawkshaw, decided to sell to yet another Irish immigrant, Patrick Flanagan.

Flanagan was determined to return his newly acquired line, now called the Flanagan and Crawly Stage, to its position of dominance; indeed, it was his intention to drive the Donnellys out of business.

Before long, violence again erupted in Biddulph Township. While no iron levers were thrown this time, William and his friends stormed the house of William Thompson in search of his daughter Margaret, whom he wanted to marry. Failing to find her, the group overran two other homes.

## The rivalry between the Donnelly Stagecoach Line and the Flanagan and Crawly Stage was escalating.

A few months later, after brothers Michael, Robert and James Jr were evicted from a lot they had been farming, the owner experienced a series of fires and death of his livestock.

Through all this, the rivalry between the Donnelly Stagecoach Line and the Flanagan and Crawly Stage was escalating. The year 1875 saw a great number of dangerous situations. William Brooks, a driver for Flanagan and Crawly, was killed when a wheel came off of his stagecoach. Shortly thereafter, a Donnelly stage was cut off by a Flanagan and Crawly employee, causing its passengers to fall to the ground. This was followed by a destructive fire at the Flanagan and Crawly stables, the burning of a Flanagan and Crawly stagecoach and the beating of Patrick Flanagan.

In that same year, Thomas was convicted of assault, William was charged with perjury and Michael was convicted of threatening the life of a rival. For a time, James Jr had the most active police file; he was accused of arson, twice accused of robbery and was convicted of assault.

Other years brought other charges. In the first three months of 1876, for example, James Jr, William, John, Patrick, Robert and Thomas together faced a total of 33 criminal charges, including: arson, assault, resisting arrest, perjury, obstructing a lawful arrest, abusive language, shooting with intent, uttering threats, robbery and theft. The town of Lucan witnessed a

riot at a wedding; more stables and stagecoaches burned; the destruction of Michael's house; the sentencing of Robert to two years imprisonment for shooting at a policeman; and the mysterious, sudden death of James Jr.

The troubled Biddulph Township was shaken further in 1879, with the arrival of a new priest, Father John Connolly, at St Patrick's Roman Catholic Church. That June, in an apparent effort to cleanse the community, Connolly formed the Biddulph Peace Society, and asked citizens to agree to searches of their homes for stolen goods. The Donnellys were the only family to refuse the priest's request. Within two months, Connolly's Society was already showing signs of strain. A splinter group known as the Vigilance Committee, featuring long-standing enemies of the Donnellys, began meeting at Biddulph's Cedar Swamp Schoolhouse. When one of their own, James Carroll, was made a constable, the Vigilance Committee

BELOW:
**William Brooks, a driver for the Flanagan and Crawly Stage, a rival of the Donnelly Stagecoach Line, was killed when a wheel came off his stagecoach.**

began acting against the Donnellys.

The last weeks leading up to the massacre saw no interruption in the long parade of dramatic events. Working on the railway in Waterford, 100 kilometres (60 miles) southeast, Michael was stabbed to death during an argument. Robert returned from Kingston Penitentiary after having served his sentence for shooting at a police constable.

On 15 January 1880, James and Johannah were accused by the Vigilance Committee of burning down the barns of Patrick 'Grouchy' Ryder, one of their old foes. Charged, the couple was to have faced a trial on 4 February. However, shortly after one o'clock that morning, approximately 30 men, many with blackened faces, walked through the falling snow and descended on James Donnelly's home. Constable Carroll is thought to have been the first to enter. He confronted and allegedly handcuffed Thomas. The mob then stormed the house. Using farm implements and clubs, they killed James and Johannah. The couple's niece, Bridget, who was visiting from Ireland, attempted to take refuge in a room upstairs, but was followed by the mob and murdered. In the mayhem, Thomas somehow managed to escape, fleeing the house. But he was quickly caught, brought back inside, and beaten to death. As the vigilantes left, they spread coal oil throughout the home and set it alight.

Witnessing all this was Johnny O'Connor, whom the family had brought in earlier in the evening to feed the livestock. The 13-year-old had survived by hiding under a bed on the main floor. Undetected, the boy managed to take flight, running to a nearby farmhouse.

The vigilantes travelled to nearby Whalen's Corners, where they surrounded William Donnelly's house. They began shouting 'Fire!' in the hope of awakening William, but succeeded instead in rousing his brother John. When the younger Donnelly appeared at the door, he was shot. William, the intended target, and his wife Nora, remained inside, hiding as John drew his last breaths.

By dawn, the curious and morbid had fallen upon James Donnelly's smouldering farmhouse, many picking through what was left for souvenirs. They had arrived in advance of the local authorities who, after minimal investigation, gathered the remains of James, Johannah, Thomas and Bridget. The four murder victims were eventually carried away in a single casket.

# By dawn, the curious and morbid had fallen upon James Donnelly's smouldering farmhouse, many picking through what was left for souvenirs.

Coroner Thomas Hossack acted with greater speed. That afternoon, he assembled a jury to begin hearing testimony at an inquest. The following day, 5 February, James Carroll and twelve other men were arrested.

On 6 February, a funeral was held for the five Donnelly dead at which Father Connolly delivered a most peculiar address, implying that the community was a better place for the murders. In this way, the priest reflected not only the thoughts of many within Biddulph Township, but those of communities further away. In reporting on the murders mere hours after they had taken place, the *St Marys Argus*, the newspaper of a picturesque town 30 kilometres (20 miles) to the east, wrote of 'the notorious family who have made their name a terror in our adjoining township.' The unknown journalist continued: 'While every person regrets that so foul a deed was perpetrated, no one regrets that the community is rid of most of a family who have made themselves a terror to the part of the country in which they resided… And while we regret exceedingly that such an atrocious murder was committed in our neighborhood, yet the people of the township of Biddulph will breathe the freer.'

The coroner's inquest continued its work through the winter. By early March, it had determined that the 'suspicious' death of the Donnellys had taken place at the hands of 'persons unknown'. Nevertheless, eight of the thirteen arrested men, Constable Carroll amongst them, had already been charged with the murders. The trial of the first accused, Carroll, thought to have been the ringleader, would not begin for eight more months. In the meantime, pressure was laid to bear on young Johnny O'Connor, the key witness in the trial. In April, the O'Connor family home was burned to the ground. The boy was moved to London, where he was placed under guard for his own protection.

There were two significant and related reasons behind the relatively long stretch of time between the massacre and the trial. The first had to do with the prosecution's unsuccessful attempt for a change of venue. It was felt that London's proximity to Lucan and the Biddulph Township would make the gathering of an unbiased jury difficult.

Influenced by Attorney General Oliver Mowat, who believed that moving the location away from the largely Catholic community would leave the government open to charges of religious discrimination, the judge refused the request. In the end, the fears of the prosecution proved to be justified when jury selection dragged

BELOW: **Roughly thirty men descended on the Donnelly house on the snowy night of 4 February 1880.**

on all the way through the summer.

The trial finally began on 4 October, and lasted just five days. As Father Connolly's controversial sermon had indicated, the verdict of the jury showed a divided community. No consensus could be reached. Seven members of the jury argued for acquittal, four were in favour of conviction, with the final juror unable to reach any decision one way or another.

## As Father Connolly's controversial sermon had indicated, the verdict of the jury showed a divided community.

It was just as the prosecution had feared. As preparations began for a second trial, which would begin on 25 January 1881, letters written by Crown Attorney Charles Hutchinson indicate a great loss of faith. He expressed considerable doubt that a conviction of even one of the accused could be obtained. Disenchantment was magnified by increasing demands for money from the O'Connor family, who seemed not to appreciate the dangerous situation in which their son had been placed.

Evidence presented at the second trial was, if anything, stronger and more substantial than at the first. And yet the prosecution, led by Aemilius Irving, Queen's Council, and former Member of Parliament, failed entirely. Where the previous effort had resulted in a hung jury, the result of this trial was out and out acquittal: after four hours of deliberation, the jury returned a verdict of 'Not guilty'.

With the Crown's second failure to convict, the remaining seven accused were all granted bail; they were never tried for the Donnelly massacre.

Curiously, for a time it appeared that there would be a third trial. Two brothers, James and William Freeheley, had fled to Michigan, where they admitted to having taken part in the massacre. Moreover, the pair claimed that Constable Carroll had also been involved in the five murders. Although the Crown was successful in extraditing the Freeheleys, it found itself unable to pursue the case when the brothers announced that they refused to testify. There is some evidence indicating that they were paid off by the Vigilance Committee.

In his 1962 book *The Donnellys Must Die*, Orlo Miller argues that the Crown came to believe that prosecution would do great damage to the community: the possibility that Father Connolly might at some point be implicated, even in the most remote manner, was considered particularly dangerous politically.

The murderers of James, Johannah, John, Thomas and Bridget Donnelly remain unidentified, thus the motives of these 'persons unknown' remains a mystery.

Some theorists have argued that the bloodbath was simply revenge for the murder of Patrick Farrell. This seems highly unlikely, as Farrell had been killed over two decades earlier. Furthermore, we are left to wonder that the extent of the killing reached far beyond Farrell's murderer to James Donnelly's wife, his niece and two of his sons. The apparent targeting of William

RIGHT:
**The story of the Donnellys has come to be used in drawing tourists to the little town of Lucan.**

LEFT:
**St Patrick's Roman Catholic Church, at which Father John Connolly gave his controversial address.**

hints that the stagecoach feud had something to do with the murders. However, it is likely that the massacre of the Donnellys was a crazed response to years of violence and crime, both actual and perceived.

In the years after Constable Carroll's acquittal, Patrick, William and Jenny (the only Donnelly daughter), left the Lucan area for nearby Glencoe. Robert remained, and in October 1881, was caught with William as they attempted to burn down a local gristmill. Incredibly, less than two years later, William was appointed a County Constable for Middlesex County, in which Biddulph is located. He never gave up hope that the murderers of his parents, brothers and cousin would one day hang.

## THE DONNELLY FAMILY

**James Donnelly**
*(1816–1880)* Father

**Johannah Magee
(or MacGee) Donnelly**
*(1823–1880)* Mother

James Donnelly, Jr
*(1842–1877)* Son

William Donnelly
*(1845–1897)* Son

**John Donnelly**
*(1847–1880)* Son

Patrick Donnelly
*(1849–1929)* Son

Michael Donnelly
*(1850–1879)* Son

Robert Donnelly
*(1853–1911)* Son

**Thomas Donnelly**
*(1854–1880)* Son

Jenny Donnelly
*(1857–1917)* Daughter

**Bridget Donnelly**
*(1858–1880)* Niece

*Names in bold indicate those
murdered on 4 February 1880.*

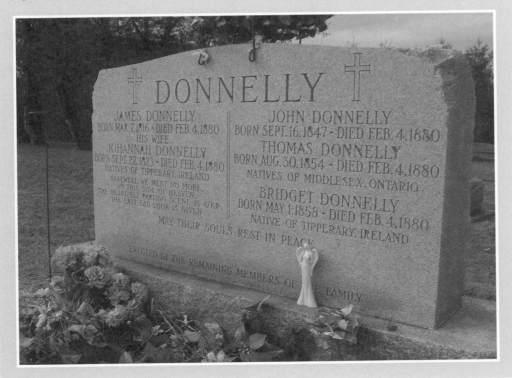

LEFT:
The grave marker that replaced the original shown on page 39. The damage has been caused by souvenir hunters who have wanted their own little piece of the stone.

# The Mad Trapper of Rat River

On 9 July 1931, a silent, somewhat stocky man arrived in Fort McPherson, a remote hamlet of 800 people, situated on the east bank of the Peel River in the Northwest Territories. There was nothing at all remarkable about Albert Johnson. A man of few words, a loner, he appeared to be well suited to a community supported largely through the solitary efforts of trapping. If Johnson stood out at all, it was because he appeared to have a considerable amount of money.

He stayed around the community for a couple of weeks, during which time he was questioned by Edgar Millen, a constable with the Royal Canadian Mounted Police.

Johnson spent what remained of the summer building a cabin on the Rat River. It was an extremely modest construction – comprising 7.5 square metres (80 square feet) in total – but had a commanding view of the surrounding countryside. The construction did not escape the attention of people within Fort McPherson. It was noted that Johnson had not bought a trapping license, yet had built his cabin in one of the very finest trapping locations on the river.

The trapping season was well underway when, in early December, several men in the area began finding that their traps had been tampered with. Suspicion immediately fell on their new neighbour Johnson. After all, there had been no similar incidents in previous years… and there had been no Albert Johnson either,

Responding to the complaints of one local trapper, on the last day of 1931, two RCMP constables, Alfred King and Joe Bernard, made their way out to Johnson's cabin. As they approached, they were pleased to see smoke coming up from the chimney, an indication that

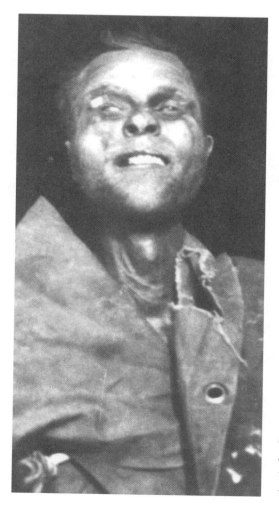

RIGHT:
**Albert Johnson's smiling corpse.**

the man they wished to question was home. However, Johnson refused to acknowledge their presence. The two constables braved bitterly cold temperatures, walking around the outside of the cabin, trying to get the inhabitant's attention. Eventually, Johnson grabbed a sack and placed it over the window. Frustrated, King and Bernard left to get a search warrant and reinforcements.

Two days later, the pair returned with two more RCMP officers and a civilian deputy. When Johnson, again, stubbornly pretended not to notice the police, King decided to enforce the search warrant. He was preparing to enter the cabin when a gunshot pierced the door. King was badly wounded. A firefight broke out, but this ended quickly when the extent of the fallen constable's injuries became evident. The four men rushed King by dogsled to Aklavik, where he eventually recovered.

In the two days that followed, a posse was assembled consisting of nine men, 42 dogs and 18 kilograms (40 pounds) of dynamite. On 4 January 1932, they moved in on Johnson's cabin. After securing the perimeter, they had to thaw out the dynamite by hugging it beneath their coats. When ready, they gathered

## King decided to enforce the search warrant. He was preparing to enter the cabin when a gunshot pierced the door.

the sticks into a single charge and tossed it through the cabin window. The resulting explosion raised the roof and brought about the collapse of one wall.

The posse entered what remained of the cabin, certain that they would find Johnson's corpse. Instead, he jumped up from a foxhole, a gun in each hand, and nearly shot two officers. The posse retreated and, after a 15-hour siege, returned to Aklavik.

News of the violence at Rat River had begun to be reported by radio stations

BELOW:
Johnson's past could be traced back no further than July 1927, when he appeared in the Yukon at Ross River for supplies, calling himself Arthur Nelson.

throughout Canada and the United States. The wanted man had been dubbed the Mad Trapper of Rat River.

Weather began to play a greater part in the story, with severe blizzards causing a delay in the return of the posse to what remained of Johnson's cabin. By the time they made it back, ten days had elapsed, and Johnson was nowhere to be found. The wanted man managed to evade his pursuers for two weeks, seemingly moving through freezing temperatures and blizzards with little difficulty. Then, on 30 January, he was surrounded at the bottom of a cliff. A firefight ensued, during which he shot and killed Edgar Millen, the RCMP constable who had interviewed him in Fort McPherson. Incredibly, though Johnson had no tools, he managed to escape by scaling a sheer cliff under cover of the night.

## Johnson had been following caribou tracks down the centre of the Eagle River, thus managing to camouflage his footprints and avoid the use of snowshoes.

It seemed that the Mad Trapper of Rat River had superhuman abilities. Inuit involved in the chase believed that Johnson could snowshoe two miles for each mile run by dogsled. Though he carried guns, he did not use them to hunt, lest they reveal his position. He lit no fires for the same reason. When the RCMP blocked two mountain passes along Johnson's route, he climbed a 2,100-metre (6,900-foot) peak by clinging to sheer cliffs of ice, and continued on his way.

In desperation, on 7 February, the RCMP brought in William 'Wop' May, the First World War flying ace, to scout the area from the sky. From his Bellanca monoplane, the aviator was able to make an observation that had eluded the pursuers. Johnson had been following caribou tracks down the centre of the Eagle River, thus managing to camouflage his footprints and avoid the use of snowshoes.

Ten days into his mission, May directed the RCMP to a bend in the Eagle River. They arrived within a few hundred metres of Johnson's position. A gun battle erupted in which Johnson seriously wounded an officer, before being shot nine times himself. He died on the spot, bringing the seven-week manhunt to an abrupt end. It seemed that the Mad Trapper of Rat River wasn't superhuman after all.

And so, Albert Johnson had been captured – or, at least, his corpse had. However, in death, he became an even more mysterious figure. In the days that followed no family member came forward to claim his body. From their initial visit to Johnson's cabin, to his death by the shore of Eagle River, not one of the people involved in the manhunt had ever heard so much as a word from Johnson's lips.

Examination of Johnson's body only raised more questions. He carried with him over 2,000 dollars in Canadian and American currency, but no identifying documentation. There was also on his person a fair quantity of gold, a knife, fishhooks, a razor, a compass, nails, a dead bird and a dead squirrel.

A dedicated search of the cabin that Johnson built revealed no photographs, no mementos – not a single item that might provide a clue as to who the Mad Trapper of Rat River was.

After all the radio coverage of the manhunt, it was to be expected that leads would flood in from amateur sleuths. The earliest names put forth were dismissed with ease. A letter arrived from an Alberta man who said he was writing on behalf of a deserted wife. Both he and the wronged woman were certain that Johnson was the husband who had fled. An enclosed photograph showed no resemblance between the two men.

Several decades later, much effort was wasted by those convinced that the Mad Trapper of Rat River was missing archaeologist Albert F. Johnson of Troy, Montana: in fact, this American Johnson was discovered to have died in 1956.

It seems that we may never know the true identity of the Mad Trapper of Rat River. There is, of course, a very real possibility that he wasn't a trapper at all. There was never any proof that Johnson had tampered with his neighbours' traps.

## A MYSTERIOUS FIGURE FICTIONALIZED

In Canada, the story of Albert Johnson has found its way into a number of works of literature, most notably Robert Kroetsch's 'Poem of Albert Johnson'. In his 1980 novel *The Mad Trapper*, Rudy Weibe portrays Albert Johnson as a man who, hurt by betrayal, had sought the solitude of Rat River.

With its action and mystery, the story of the 1932 manhunt seems well suited for the screen. Indeed, Weibe's *The Mad Trapper* was adapted from a script to a movie that was never made. Hollywood has twice made feature films centred on Johnson's story.

The 1975 *Challenge to Be Free* takes a great number of liberties with Johnson's story, including transporting the setting to the United States. In the film, Johnson lives a near utopian existence in harmony with the animals that surround him. His problems begin when he comes upon traps that employ inhumane techniques. He accidentally shoots a policeman, which results in a two-week manhunt through the Alaskan wilderness, culminating in a fuzzy ending in which the trapper appears to commit suicide.

In the 1981 film *Death Hunt*, Charles Bronson portrays Johnson as an American veteran of the First World War, who finds himself on the wrong side of a group of cruel and ignorant trappers. Setting the action in the Yukon, the screenwriters departed from the true story in many significant ways, including the level of carnage. Edgar Millen, the young RCMP constable who Johnson killed, is advanced in age and rank. Played by 57-year-old Lee Marvin, he becomes Sergeant Edgar Millen, the commander of the local RCMP post. 'Wop' May, whose skills contributed greatly to the manhunt, is replaced by the fictional Captain Hank Tucker, a trigger-happy pilot with the Royal Canadian Air Force. A threat to the men on the ground, Tucker is killed after the RCMP shoot his plane from the sky. The film ends with Johnson's escape into Alaska.

ABOVE LEFT: Charles Bronson as Albert Johnson in the 1981 Hollywood feature *Death Hunt*.

# He Who Flies By Night

ABOVE:
**Grey Owl in buckskin and *ceinture fleche*.**

ABOVE RIGHT: **A poster for Buffalo Bill's Wild West Show, in which Grey Owl claimed to have performed.**

Grey Owl was a commanding presence. He stood at an inch or two over six feet (about 1.8 metres). Invariably dressed in buckskin and moccasins, the Indian had a quiet dignity about him. World famous, the greatest conservationist of his time, he never made any attempt to hide his humble origins. Grey Owl wrote that he was the son of a Scotsman, George MacNeill, and Katherine Cochise, an Apache from the Jacarillo band. A simple, contented couple, they had had their encounters with the rich and famous. George had served as a scout for his good friend William 'Buffalo Bill' Cody. Both parents had spent much of 1887 performing in England as players in Buffalo Bill's Wild West Show tour, made in celebration of Queen Victoria's Golden Jubilee. In Grey Owl's account, when his parents began their voyage back across the Atlantic, his mother was with child. It might be said in more ways than one that Grey Owl was conceived in England.

Grey Owl said that he'd been born in 1888 at Hermosillo, Mexico, some 200 kilometres (125 miles) south of the American border. Shortly thereafter, his family began moving north until they reached the Great Plains, where he was raised as an Apache. In early adolescence Grey Owl followed in his parents' footsteps by performing as a knife thrower in their old friend Buffalo Bill's Wild West Show.

At the age of 15, he made his way to Western Canada, seeking work as a wilderness guide in territory with which he had no familiarity. In 1903, stories of a silver strike in the north Ontario town of Cobalt sent him farther east. However, he never did become a miner or a prospector, preferring instead to support himself through trapping and occasional work as a guide.

Grey Owl lived a modest life, entirely unnoticed. Then, quite by chance, he

LEFT:
**The young Grey Owl, then an English schoolboy known as Archibald Belaney.**

became a writer, sharing his love of nature and message of conservationism through books and magazine articles. Fame followed, and the Indian soon became known as a great orator.

The pinnacle of this second career came in 1937, when he gave a royal command performance before George VI and Queen Elizabeth. In meeting the King, Grey Owl spoke first in the Ojibway language; only after he had finished did the Indian provide the monarch with a translation.

Three months later, he was dead.

The newspapers had tended to ignore Grey Owl's claim that his father was a Scot – and never did write about his blue eyes – preferring to portray him as a full-blooded Indian. Upon his death, obituary writers told of a man who had been an inspiration to all. The *New York*

*Times* paid tribute to Grey Owl, describing him as a man who 'would have gotten on well with Thoreau, though, curiously enough, Grey Owl was far more sentimental than Thoreau, the French-descended New Englander'.

However, one obituary was something less than complimentary. In reporting Grey Owl's death, the *Toronto Star* broke the story that the conservationist wasn't an Indian at all. His true name wasn't Grey Owl, but Archibald Stansfeld Belaney. He was not born in the Mexican city of Hermosillo, but in an English port city, where he had been raised by his grandmother and two spinster aunts, Ada and Carrie. The man known as Grey Owl had turned 18 years of age before he first set eyes on the shores of North America.

BELOW:
**Nineteenth century trappers. Grey Owl continued the tradition in the 20th century.**

The revelation brought something of a mixed reaction from the press. While news of Grey Owl's secret identity was most certainly the sort of sensational story that sold papers, editors and journalists hated the idea of exposing themselves as having been so gullible. They had been fooled by a man who not only wasn't an Indian, but wasn't even North American.

The initial bombshell set forth a flood of researchers who devoted themselves to unravelling the many mysteries of Grey Owl's life. It wasn't long before the man's *œuvre* became dwarfed by biographies and critical studies. Each new book, it seemed, contained further revelations.

Archibald Belaney told the truth in writing that he'd been born in 1888 – the precise date was 18 September – however, it is from this point that fact and fantasy diverge.

His parents were not at all like the devoted couple he had described in his writing. Belaney had been born to a mother who, it is thought, may have been as young as 13 years old. For a time his father had a great deal of money, inherited from his family, but he squandered it all on drink and other women. In 1901, following the break-up of their marriage, Belaney's father left the country. He was later killed in a bar-room brawl.

Long before this seemingly inevitable dissolution took place, the future conservationist had been placed in the care of his grandmother and two aunts. Archibald Belaney was sent to Hastings Grammar School, a 300-year-old institution, where it was hoped he would learn the self-discipline that had so eluded his father. An introspective child, young Belaney had no friends to speak of and devoted his leisure time to the study of nature. He also demonstrated a keen interest in the history and culture of 'Red Indians'.

By 1906, Belaney had had enough of his aunts and their plans for his future. Somehow he managed to convince his Aunt Ada to send him to Toronto. Belaney had said he would study agriculture, but it is now obvious that his true goal was to become a 'wilderness man'.

The story he later told as Grey Owl, about having been attracted by the silver strike in Cobalt, has some basis in fact. From Toronto, Belaney started out on the 500-kilometre (300-mile) trek to the northern mining town – an effort that very nearly cost him his life as his knowledge of the bush and survival skills was limited to what he had picked up from books like Ernest Thompson Seton's *Two Little Savages* that he'd read as an English schoolboy. However, Providence smiled favourably, and he encountered a woodsman named Jesse Hood who, with a band of Ojibway, nursed him back to health. With the knowledge garnered from his new friends, Belaney adapted well to the bush. For nearly nine years, he remained in the remote north, supporting himself through trapping beaver and occasional employment as a wilderness guide and forest ranger.

## The initial bombshell set forth a flood of researchers who devoted themselves to unravelling the many mysteries of Grey Owl's life.

It took the advent of the First World War to draw Belaney out of the bush. His attestation papers for the Canadian Over-Seas Expeditionary Force reveal his tendency for, and skills in, fabrication; Belaney reported that he'd been born in Montreal and that he had once served with the 'Mexican Scouts, 28th Dragoons'.

By enlisting Belaney had made the worst mistake of his life. Sent overseas, he was subjected to the horrors of trench warfare. His lungs were seared with mustard gas and he received a serious wound to the foot. Chewed up

RIGHT:
**The horrors of trench warfare.**

by the war machine, he returned to the Ontario north a bitter, scarred man.

He fought and drank to a point at which complete self-destruction seemed inevitable. However, Belaney was again saved by the Ojibway. Under the guidance of Neganikabu, a tribal elder, he took part in manhood rituals and, as Wa-sha-quon-asin – 'He who flies by night' – was adopted into the tribe.

Though invariably described as a rebirth, the experience also served to restore much of the Archibald Belaney who had existed before going off to war. He soon reversed the damage done to his reputation, and again found employment as a wilderness guide.

In the summer of 1925, while working in the Temagami, between North Bay and Cobalt, he had a chance encounter with Anahareo, a young Mohawk woman 18 years his junior. The following winter, she came to live in his cabin.

Anahareo's appearance in Belaney's life coincided with his conversion from trapper of beavers to devoted conservationist, a personal transformation he described in his 1934 autobiography, *Pilgrims of the Wild*. Belaney writes that the winter of Anahareo's arrival had proved particularly bad for trapping, and he was left with no choice but to undertake a spring hunt. He had avoided such hunts in the past, recognizing that spring trapping invariably left many newborn beaver kittens orphaned; this, in turn, would cause a decline in the beaver population.

During the hunt, when he and Anahareo came across two orphaned beaver kittens, Belaney realized immediately that he had killed the mother. The experience left him with such distaste that he vowed to give up trapping beaver and dedicate himself to establishing a sanctuary for the rodent. With Anahareo, he adopted the two beaver kittens and as the self-proclaimed President of the Society of the Beaver People, relocated to Quebec's Birch Lake, near the border with New Brunswick.

At first, Belaney's grand project appeared destined for failure. The refuge had been establishing in an area that featured few fur-bearing animals, and he felt pressured to break his vow not to hunt beaver.

In the midst of this bleak-looking situation, he began setting down on paper his thoughts and observations on the adopted beavers and the surrounding wilderness. Pressure on Belaney's finances was alleviated somewhat when these were sold through his mother to England's *Country Life* magazine. Although he had no inkling, Belaney was now set on

ABOVE:
**Grey Owl's cabin on Saskatchewan's Lake Ajawaan.**

a course that would lead ultimately to the bestseller lists and international fame as a conservationist.

He recognized early on that his message would receive more attention if it appeared to come from a 'native' viewpoint. And so the 'A. S. Belaney' who had made his debut in *Country Life* became 'Grey Owl'. In order to appear Indian, he coloured his skin with henna and died his long braided hair black.

The last eight years of his life was marked by a period of exhausting activity. Grey Owl wrote four books, numerous magazine articles, and began a career in public speaking. Supported by the federal government, he established a beaver sanctuary in Manitoba's Riding Mountain National Park, then moved the colony to a new refuge in Saskatchewan at Lake Ajawaan in Prince Albert National Park. He toured Canada, the United States and Europe, appeared in films and shared his ideas on conservationism with some of the most powerful men on the continent.

However, in the midst of this success life had begun to sour. Anahareo left, taking with her their daughter. Increasingly, he found himself called away from his cabin on Lake Ajawaan and the wilderness in which he thrived.

A 1937 speaking tour of Great Britain, his second in two years, was a terrible mistake. Delivered over a three-month period, the 138 lectures drained his energy. He returned to Canada a frail man. 'Another month of this lecturing will kill me', he told attendant reporters. 'I must return to my cabin in Saskatchewan.' The homecoming was

indeed in the plans, but he was first expected to speak on a 12-week lecture tour of North America.

Grey Owl succeeded in making it back to his home on Lake Ajawaan, but the stay was brief. He fell suddenly ill with pneumonia and was taken by horse-drawn sleigh to the hospital. By the end of the second day, he had fallen into a coma. The next morning he was dead.

Grey Owl's life is slowly coming together, yet certain questions remain unanswered. Was his mother really 13 when she gave birth? Exactly how many wives, common-law or otherwise, did he have? Was he a bigamist?

There is one more mystery that stumps 21st-century Canadians: how is it that for so long Grey Owl was able to fool people into believing that he was an Indian?

That those who turned out to see the man speak accepted that he was an Indian is, perhaps, understandable. Simply put, Grey Owl fit the image of what people had come to believe Indians were. Lloyd Roberts, the son of novelist Sir Charles G. D. Roberts, said that Grey Owl was, 'the first Indian that really looked like an Indian – an Indian from those thrilling Wild West days of covered wagons, buffalos and Sitting Bulls.'

But what of the First Nation people? They had invited Grey Owl to speak at conferences devoted to their concerns. Though nearly all who saw him recognized the conservationist's masquerade, he was not exposed as a fraud. Perhaps this is because so very few viewed the Englishman as an impostor. After all, as Wa-sha-quon-asin, Archibald Belaney had been

ABOVE:
Anahareo with one of
the beavers she and
Grey Owl had come to
protect.

adopted into the Ojibway. He had undergone the rites expected of any other male member of the tribe. There was no question that this blue-eyed Englishman was now one of them. Many in the other First Nations accepted Grey Owl because of his adoption by the Ojibway. Still others raised no objection for the simple reason that he was such an effective spokesperson on issues that they held dear.

## A WRITER IN SEARCH OF HIMSELF

The 1930s were a time when very few books by Canadian writers were being published. In this environment, Grey Owl found himself part of an exclusive club that included Stephen Leacock and Mazo de la Roche. Another contemporary, Frederick Philip Grove, author of *Over Prairie Trails* and *Settlers of the Marsh*, was considered to be one of the finest writers Canada had ever produced. While it was true that he had not been born a Canadian, it wasn't until after he immigrated in 1912 that his first work was published. He wrote openly about his early life in Sweden, and the journey that eventually brought him to Canada, in his autobiography *In Search of Myself*. A commercial and critical success, it earned Grove a 1946 Governor-General's Award for English Language Non-fiction. It was the last title published during the author's lifetime; Grove died two years later, not long before what would have been his 70th birthday.

After his death, Grove continued to be read and studied. Four of his works were republished as part of the New Canadian Library series and, in 1971, a new volume of short stories was published. In October of that very same year, D. O. Spettigue, a professor at Queen's University, made a startling discovery: Frederick Philip Grove was really Felix Paul Greve, a minor literary figure in early 20th-century Munich and Berlin.

Grove was not Swedish, as he had claimed, rather he had been born in Randomno, West Prussia. He wrote essays, plays, poems and novels, but is best remembered as the man whose translations first introduced the works of Oscar Wilde, André Gide, H. G. Wells and Algernon Charles Swinburne to German readers.

This whirlwind of literary activity was matched by a stormy personal life. Moving around Berlin, Grove – or Greve – stole another man's wife, was imprisoned for defrauding a friend out of a large sum of money, and in 1904 agreed voluntary exile in Switzerland and France. He later returned to Berlin where, in 1909, Greve faked his suicide in order to escape debt and other obligations.

For a time, the revelation that one of the most studied writers in the country had had a secret life, not to mention a previously unknown body of work, created even more interest in Grove. However, the past couple of decades have not treated Grove well. He is seldom read outside the world of academia and his novels are often dismissed as bland and uninteresting. It would seem that Frederick Philip Grove's greatest work of fiction was himself.

ABOVE RIGHT: Frederick Philip Grove, when he was known as Felix Paul Greve.

# CHAPTER 3:
# THE DISAPPEARED

# Sir John Franklin, the *Terror* and the *Erebus*

Of all the mysteries in Canadian history, that surrounding the fate of Sir John Franklin and his 128 gallant men dominates. The story of their ill-fated expedition runs through the culture, inspiring such diverse works as Gwendolyn McEwan's verse play *Terror and Erebus* and *Solomon Gursky Was Here* by Mordecai Richler.

At the centre of the mystery are HMS *Terror* and HMS *Erebus*. Barque-rigged bomb vessels, weighing between 326 and 378 tons, both had been designed for war. Indeed, the *Terror* had seen service in the War of 1812. She had participated in the 1814 Battle of Baltimore, the attack that had inspired Francis Scott Key to compose *The Star-Spangled Banner*.

The strength of the vessels made them well suited to Arctic service. The *Terror* had endured an ill-fated 1836 expedition to Hudson's Bay. Ice had forced the ship 12 metres (40 feet) up the side of a cliff, and on the return journey she had struck an iceberg, yet the strength of the *Terror* had ensured her survival. Accompanied by the *Erebus*, in 1840 she began a successful three-year expedition to the Antarctic.

These adventures appeared extremely modest in scope when compared to the

ABOVE LEFT:
**Sir John Franklin. Born at Spilsby, Lincolnshire, England, he died off the coast of King William Island.**

ABOVE:
**An imaginative depiction of HMS *Terror* and HMS *Erebus* in the Arctic Ocean.**

expedition under the leadership of Sir John Franklin. The voyages planned for the *Terror* and *Erebus* were to take them through the largely uncharted labyrinth of islands in the frigid waters of the Canadian north. They would then leave the Arctic Ocean through the Bering Strait, proceed to the Sandwich Islands and return to England after rounding Cape Horn. The grand objectives of the expedition were the discovery and conquer of the elusive Northwest Passage. This supposed northern shortcut between Europe and Asia had been sought for centuries without success. However, as the 19th century progressed, many in the Royal Navy believed that with recent advances in knowledge and equipment the goal would soon be achieved.

In preparation for the expedition, the *Terror* and *Erebus* had been fitted with the latest in Victorian technology. Both were installed with steam engines, thus enabling the vessels to reach a speed of up to four knots under their own power. Iron wells were also constructed, which allowed for the retraction of propellers and rudders so as to protect them from the ice.

With full knowledge that passage through the Arctic would be long and arduous, the Admiralty focused on the comfort of the crews. A steam heating system was constructed onboard, and three years' supply of preserved food was supplied. A library of over 1,000 books, including Oliver Goldsmith's *The Vicar of Wakefield*, so popular amongst Victorians, was also included.

The final voyage of the *Terror* and the *Erebus* began on the morning of 19 May 1845, when they left the village of Greenhithe, 25 kilometres (15 miles) east of London, England. They sailed toward the mouth of the River Thames and then headed north to the Orkney Islands in northern Scotland. In July the expedition reached the west coast of Greenland, where they received fresh provisions. Later that same month, the ships encountered the whalers *Enterprise* and *Prince of Wales* in the sea between Greenland and Baffin Island. It would be the last contact that the *Terror* and the *Erebus* would have with the European world.

For the British Admiralty, Franklin's expedition turned mysterious as it entered its third year. There had been no word from the expedition since July 1845, when the ship had sent papers from Greenland. Reacting to public pressure, in the spring of 1848 the Royal Navy dispatched three rescue expeditions. An overland rescue party – led by explorer and naturalist John Rae – travelled down the Mackenzie River to the Canadian Arctic coast, and was complemented by two other expeditions by sea. One gained the Canadian Arctic from the Atlantic, while the other entered through the Bering Strait.

A reward of £20,000 was offered 'to any Party or Parties, of any country, who shall render assistance to the crews of the Discovery Ships under the command of Sir John Franklin'.

After the rescue expeditions found no trace of the *Terror* or the *Erebus* and their respective crews and the award money lay unclaimed, the mystery only deepened.

More than two dozen major search expeditions were conducted in the decades that followed. In 1850, one of the more active years, 11 British and two American vessels sailed the Canadian Arctic in search of Franklin and his men. This concentrated effort led to the discovery of the first relics on Beechey Island, including the graves of the first three crewmembers to die. The mystery remained, however, as no documentation was found on the site.

## A reward of £20,000 was offered 'to any Party or Parties, of any country, who shall render assistance to the crews of the Discovery Ships under the command of Sir John Franklin'.

Four years later, John Rae, the explorer who had led the failed overland rescue mission of 1848, uncovered further signs of Sir John Franklin's expedition. While surveying the Boothia Peninsula, the northernmost point of the North American mainland, for the Hudson's Bay Company, he met an Inuit man who spoke of several dozen *qallunaat* (Inuktitut for 'white men') who had starved to death near the

BELOW: **One skeleton from the Franklin Expedition, discovered in 1859.**

RIGHT: **The body of John Torrington, who died 1 January 1846, less than eight months into the expedition.**

mouth of the Back River. Rae was shown several items from the expedition. From other Inuit he purchased silver cutlery that was later identified as belonging to various officers, including Franklin himself.

At the urging of the Admiralty, members of the Hudson's Bay Company investigated further. In the spring and summer of 1855, Chief Factor James Anderson and another employee journeyed north to the mouth of the Back River. On the way they came across a group of Inuit, who repeated the story of the *qallunaat* who had died of starvation along the northern coast. Weeks later, the pair came across a piece of wood on the northern Montreal Island, inscribed *'Erebus'* and *'Mr Stanley'* – almost certainly a reference to Stephen S. Stanley, the ship's surgeon.

Coming just over a decade after the *Terror* and the *Erebus* sailed out of Greenhithe and along the Thames, the important discoveries made by Anderson and his partner appeared to confirm what had long been suspected, that Sir John Franklin and the rest of the men of the expedition were dead.

However, not everyone was willing to abandon hope. Lady Franklin petitioned the government, asking for yet another search expedition. When unsuccessful, she herself commissioned just such a mission led by Irish explorer Sir Francis Leopold McClintock. In the summer of 1857, the expedition sailed from Aberdeen on the steam schooner *Fox*. McClintock and his men were nearly two years into their mission when they came upon a document – a single sheet of paper – on King William Island. Composed by Francis Crozier, executive officer and commander of the *Terror*, and James Fitzjames, commander of the *Erebus*, it recorded that Franklin and 23 other members of the expedition had died. Several skeletons were discovered, along with a number of relics, including silk handkerchiefs, scented soap, slippers and hair combs.

ABOVE :
**The fate of the
Franklin Expedition,
as imagined in the
18th century.**

Further expeditions, conducted during the following years, discovered graves and abandoned campgrounds. For a time, the optimistic held out hope that at least some of the men would be found living among the Inuit. However, this proved increasingly unlikely, particularly given reports coming from hunters who had witnessed members of the expedition walking southwards. The Inuit told McClintock that the *qallunaat* had resorted to cannibalism.

The last in the line of searches for relics of the Franklin Expedition took place over a two-year period, beginning in 1878. Led by American explorer Frederick Schwatka, the mission focused on known and likely sites, in the hope that the official records of the Franklin Expedition might be found. The failure to uncover the documentation prompted Schwatka to claim that they were lost forever.

Over a century passed before there would be another expedition of any significance. In 1981, a group of scientists led by Canadian anthropologist Owen Beattie began a series of scientific studies of the remains found on Beechey and King William islands. Their work, which employed the techniques of modern forensics, revealed evidence of scurvy, pneumonia, tuberculosis, lead poisoning and cannibalism.

The work of recent decades, combined with the searches undertaken during the 19th century, have solved much of the mystery as to what actually happened to Franklin and his men.

We now know that in the summer and early autumn of 1845, the expedition circumnavigated Cornwallis Island before heading to Beechey Island. There the men wintered, three of their number dying. After the spring thaw, the *Terror* and the *Erebus* made their way south, down Peel Sound. On 12 September 1846, they became trapped in ice off the northern coast of King William Island. The crew wintered on the island, expecting that come the spring and summer the ships would be freed. However, this did not happen. The *Terror* and the *Erebus* remained locked in ice. They would never sail again. On 11 June 1847, Franklin died. On 26 April 1848, after their third winter in the Arctic – and the second winter spent locked in ice off the coast of King William Island – the surviving crew decided to walk toward the Canadian mainland. When the men set

**The crew wintered on the island, expecting that come the spring and summer the ships would be freed. However, this did not happen.**

out on their trek, their number had already been reduced by two dozen. Most of the 105 men who had been fortunate to have survived thus far would die on the island. Although some 30 or 40 souls would reach the mainland, all would perish many hundreds of kilometres from the nearest European outpost at Great Bear Lake.

Much of the failure of the ill-fated expedition can be attributed to Franklin's decision to pass down the western side of King William Island. Until recent years, the ice on this side of the island did not always clear in the summer. While the eastern side would have been a better choice, Franklin had no evidence to indicate that the landmass was not a peninsula. It is not coincidental that when finally conquering the Northwest Passage in his expedition of 1903 to 1905, Norwegian explorer Roald Amundsen sailed down the eastern side of the island.

Another key factor in the failure of the Franklin Expedition is the certainty that many, if not all of the men, suffered from lead poisoning. The source of this horrible affliction can be traced back to a man named Stephen Goldner, who was awarded the contract to supply 8,000 tinned preserves. The shoddy work in applying the lead soldering caused the deadly metal to enter the food. The ships' water systems are also suspected of introducing lead into the diets of the crewmembers.

With documentation limited to the single sheet of paper bearing messages from Francis Crozier and James Fitzjames, we cannot know what occurred during the last voyage of the *Terror* and the *Erebus*, and we are left to speculate as to what life was like for their crews once the ships had become locked in ice. However, there are some who have pointed to this absence of documentation as evidence of conspiracy. Might it be that the Royal Navy, having found evidence of madness and cannibalism, suppressed the expedition's official records?

Perhaps the boldest of all conspiracy theories concerning the expedition has it that Sir John Franklin was, in fact, successful in sailing the Northwest Passage. The truth, it would seem, is found on a monument found in Spilsbury, Lincolnshire, the explorer's birthplace. Below his likeness is found the inscription 'Sir John Franklin – Discoverer of the North West Passage.'

## LADY FRANKLIN'S LAMENT

The Franklin Expedition has been the subject of numerous folk songs, including the Fairport Convention's *I'm Already There* and, most famously, *Northwest Passage* by Stan Rogers. The earliest-known song, *Lady Franklin's Lament*, also known as *Lord Franklin*, dates back to 1855, ten years after the *Erebus* and the *Terror* set sail from England:

**Lady Franklin's Lament**

*The other night on the rolling deep*
*While in my hammock I fell asleep.*
*I dreamed a dream and I thought it true,*
*Concerning Franklin and his gallant crew.*

*With a hundred seamen he sailed away,*
*To the frozen ocean in the month of May,*
*To seek that passage beyond the pole,*
*Where we poor seamen do sometimes go.*

*Through cruel hardships they vainly strove,*
*Their ships on mountains of ice were drove,*
*Where the Eskimo in his skin canoe*
*Is the only one who ever came through.*

*In Baffin's Bay where the whale-fish blow,*
*The fate of Franklin no man may know.*
*The fate of Franklin no tongue can tell,*
*Lord Franklin along with his sailors do dwell.*

*And now my memory it gives me pain,*
*For my long-lost Franklin I'd cross the main.*
*Ten thousand pounds would I freely give*
*To know on earth, that my Franklin do live.*

# The Final Voyage of the *Mary Celeste*

LEFT:
**The *Mary Celeste*
when it was known as
the *Amazon*.**

In 1884, three years before the first appearance of Sherlock Holmes, Arthur Conan Doyle wrote a story entitled 'J. Habakuk Jephson's Statement'. Published anonymously in *Cornhill Magazine*, the young writer received £30 for his effort. Doyle's tale was based loosely on the mystery of the *Mary Celeste*, a sound vessel that had been found abandoned in the Atlantic Ocean. It was most certainly not a unique occurrence. In 1849, the *Hermania*, a Dutch Schooner, was discovered floating without its captain, his family, or his crew. Another ship, *Marathon*, was found in a similar state six years later. While the *Hermania* and *Marathon* are forgotten, the *Mary Celeste* lives on in public consciousness because of Doyle's story. Indeed, the ghost ship is frequently referred to as

the '*Marie Celeste*' – just one of several liberties the author took in order to make for a better tale.

The *Mary Celeste* was a brigantine – a ship with two masts, the forward of which is square rigged. Once a preferred vessel of pirates, she was of a type commonly used as merchant ships.

The *Mary Celeste* hadn't enjoyed a trouble-free history. She was the first vessel built on Spencer's Island, near the head of the Bay of Fundy. Launched under the name *Amazon* in May of 1861, her first captain died less than 48 hours into her maiden voyage. She later collided with another ship in the English Channel, causing it to sink.

The years that followed were relatively uneventful but then, in 1867, the brigantine was driven aground during a storm off Cow Bay, Cape

Breton. The two men who attempted to salvage her were bankrupted by their efforts. The *Amazon* eventually ended up in New York, where she was sold in a public auction for $10,000. The new owner, an American, had her refitted at a cost of $11,500. Before work was completed she was sold a second time and was rechristened – believed by sailors to be an unlucky thing to do – the *Mary Celeste*.

The brigantine enjoyed five more profitable, uneventful years before coming under the command of Captain Benjamin Briggs. An American, Briggs had spent much of his 37 years at sea, and had previously captained three different vessels, including another brigantine, *Sea Foam*. At one point, the captain had seriously considered giving up his seafaring ways. In 1871, he very nearly traded his vocation to lead a less

RIGHT: **New Englander Benjamin Briggs, captain of the *Mary Celeste.***

LEFT: **David Reed Morehouse, captain of the *Dei Gratia*, the ship that discovered the *Mary Celeste*.**

adventurous life as the owner of a hardware store in New Bedford, Connecticut. However, something had encouraged Briggs to continue his career. Early the next year, he bought eight of 24 shares in the *Mary Celeste* and had the cabin modified to house his family.

The mysterious final voyage of the *Mary Celeste* began on 5 November 1872, when the ship, carrying a cargo of 1,701 barrels of alcohol valued at $35,000, set sail from New York Harbor for Genoa, Italy. Briggs was

accompanied by his wife, his two-year-old daughter and a crew of seven.

There was trouble from the start. The ship was forced to spend nearly two days anchored off Staten Island, waiting for heavy seas to subside. On the morning of 7 November, the *Mary Celeste* resumed her journey. For Captain Briggs, his family and his crew, the sights witnessed that day would be their last of North America.

Twenty-seven days later, on 4 December, the *Mary Celeste* was sighted, sailing erratically, by the *Dei Gratia*, some 900 kilometres (550 miles) off Gibraltar. The latter vessel had also left from New York, some eight days after the *Mary Celeste*. After a couple of hours' observation, during which no signs of activity were detected, the commander of the *Dei Gratia*, Captain David Reed Morehouse, ordered a small party to board the *Mary Celeste*.

According to the first mate, Oliver Deveau, what the men discovered was a mystery. Briggs, his wife, his daughter, and all seven crewmembers were nowhere to be found. Though there was water between decks, and over a metre (3 feet) more in the hold, the *Mary Celeste* was in good condition overall. While there were no overt signs of foul play, a few peculiarities were

> **Flood developed a theory that Briggs' crew had been at the alcohol, had murdered the captain and his family, and had cut some sort of deal with the crew of the *Dei Gratia*.**

discovered. The clock and compass had been broken. The sextant, marine chronometer and navigation book were missing. Though the ship's register and papers were nowhere to be found, the captain's logbook remained – the final entry, made 24 November, provided no indication of anything out of the ordinary. Finally, the brigantine's sole lifeboat appeared to have been launched, suggesting that the *Mary Celeste* had been abandoned intentionally.

On 12 December, crewmen from the *Dei Gratia* sailed the *Mary Celeste* into the Port of Gibraltar, where they laid a claim against the owners, Briggs included, for salvage. There, before the Vice Admiralty Court, they met with two very different receptions. While the presiding justice, Sir James Cochrane, praised the crew of the *Dei Gratia*

for their bravery and skill, the Queen's Proctor, Frederick Solly Flood, suspected the same men of foul play.

Flood's suspicions had been aroused when he'd heard a crewmember from the *Dei Gratia* describe the *Mary Celeste* as being 'fit to sail around the world with good crew and good sails.' He ordered a survey that failed to uncover evidence of any wrongdoing. Unsatisfied, Flood ordered a second survey, and was frustrated when it provided similar findings.

Flood developed a theory that Briggs' crew had been at the alcohol, had murdered the captain and his family, and had cut some sort of deal with the crew of the *Dei Gratia*. Unsatisfied, he proposed a second scenario involving a conspiracy hatched between Briggs and Morehouse. Ultimately, although the Queen's Proctor could prove nothing, he did manage to sway the court. The amount awarded the crew of the *Dei Gratia* was much less than in comparable cases. Morehouse, their captain, received one-fifth the value of the ship and its cargo.

The *Mary Celeste* met a rather ignoble end. A little over 12 years later, on 3 January 1885, she ran up on the Rochelois Reef off Haiti. A subsequent insurance investigation uncovered fraud. In 2001, novelist and marine archaeologist Clive Cussler announced that he had found the remains of the *Mary Celeste*, although his claim was later challenged after recovered wood fragments proved inconsistent with tree ring dating.

While the exact location of the *Mary Celeste* remains a matter under dispute, its fate is well documented. The same cannot be said for Briggs, his family and his crew. Their mysterious disappearance, seemingly without a trace, has prompted over thirteen decades of speculation.

Perhaps the earliest theory, first proposed during the proceedings of the Vice Admiralty Court, suggests that the missing people were victims of piracy.

However, while it is true that pirates then operated in the waters the *Mary Celeste* sailed, the ship bore no signs of any struggle or conflict. Moreover, the cargo, the only thing of value on the ship, remained largely untouched.

A number of theories, including that suggested by Flood, had it that the *Dei Gratia* caught up with the *Mary Celeste* and killed all aboard so that they might apply for salvage rights. Doing so at sea, the murderous crew would have likely had a good deal of time to dispose of the bodies and wash down the ship of blood or any other signs of struggle. An alternate version of this theory has it that Morehouse, who was an acquaintance of the missing captain, placed at least three of his own men on the ship – enough, perhaps, to overtake the vessel and murder all on board.

The most simple explanation provided by those claiming to have solved the mystery is that all ten souls aboard the *Mary Celeste* were simply swept overboard, presumably along with the ship's register, papers, sextant, chronometer and navigation book.

The most fanciful of the stories envisions the *Mary Celeste* coming to the aid of a burning cargo ship filled with coal and explosives. According to this scenario the *Mary Celeste* then ventured too close to the burning vessel, causing Briggs, his family and his crew to abandon ship. They then used their lifeboat to pick up the crew of the cargo ship. In the end, all effort proved futile – the lifeboat capsized and all souls were lost. This fairly elaborate theory ignores the fact that there is no record of a cargo ship being lost during that period.

The most likely theories rely on the discovery that nine of the 1,701 barrels of alcohol carried by the *Mary Celeste* were found to be empty.

Noting that Briggs was a devout man and a staunch abstainer, many theorists posit that the good captain discovered his crew drinking from the barrels, a fight then ensued, and the trouble grew from there.

This led to a theory that was first proposed by James Winchester, the ship's main shareholder. It is possible that the barrels leaked, causing an explosion. This would explain the report from the *Dei Gratia* that the hold doors were found open. Indeed, an experiment conducted at University College London in 2006 indicated that the ignition of the alcohol's vapour would have blown open the doors to the hold, but would not have left burn marks.

ABOVE:
**One of the many theories about the fate of the crew is that they were simply swept overboard.**

Those who promote this theory believe that in the aftermath of such an explosion, Briggs would have ordered all onboard into the lifeboat. If true, he

## In the aftermath of an explosion, Briggs would have ordered all onboard into the lifeboat.

would have most certainly secured the lifeboat to the *Mary Celeste* with a strong towline. Indeed, when found by the *Dei Gratia*, a frayed rope, seven centimetres (three inches) in circumference, was discovered trailing behind the ship. The records of the Servico Metrologico in the Azores, the closest weather station, indicate that the area had experienced a storm in the days preceding the discovery of the *Mary Celeste*.

A related theory has it that Briggs had the hold opened, detected the noxious fumes and, panicking, ordered all into the lifeboat.

## *THE MYSTERY OF THE* MARIE CELESTE

A dramatic, if unfounded account concerning the fate of those onboard the ghost ship is featured in *The Mystery of the Marie Celeste*, a 1935 film starring Béla Lugosi. In the film Briggs and Morehouse are not mere acquaintances, but best friends. Morehouse is in love with a young woman called Sarah, and is eager to show her off to Briggs in New York. Of course, Briggs also falls in love with Sarah – and she with him. Both suitors end up proposing on the same day. Sarah chooses Briggs and Morehouse becomes angry and is consumed by jealousy. When he confronts Briggs, Morehouse is told that the rival captain will marry Sarah, even if it brings about the end of their friendship.

After their marriage, the couple prepare to sail on the *Marie Celeste*. Briggs, who is short on crew, asks his old friend for help. Morehouse offers up Volkerk Grot, who works on the ship to get it ready for sailing, but is not onboard when it sails. Briggs himself manages to recruit some men, amongst them Anton Lorenzen, a sailor of fragile mental health played by Lugosi.

The *Marie Celeste* sets sail. Before long the crew realizes that there is a murderer onboard. Slowly, one by one, they are falling victim. A crewmember attempts to rape Sarah. The assailant is killed by Lorenzen, who then breaks down at the thought of having taken a human life. It isn't long before nearly everybody on the ship has died or disappeared, including Sarah and Briggs. The only people left are Lorenzen, First Mate Wilson, and a third crewmember named Katz. The trio recognize that they will soon discover who of their number is the killer.

After coming to the conclusion that the sensitive Lorenzen could not kill, Katz attacks Wilson. The First Mate shoots Katz and then celebrates his becoming the new captain of the *Marie Celeste*. Lorenzen becomes angry, telling Wilson that he was forced to work on the ship six years before and had been murdering those onboard in revenge.

He shoots Wilson and then throws him into the ocean. Having done so, he starts wandering the *Marie Celeste* in search of the man he has just killed. Increasingly frantic and frenzied, Lorenzen finally jumps off the deck to his death.

In an enigmatic final scene, Morehouse is shown giving Grot a large amount of money.

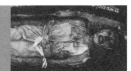

# Ambrose Small Exits the Stage

'All thieves must plan their escape routes.' So declares millionaire Ambrose Small in Michael Ondaatje's 1987 novel *In the Skin of a Lion*.

Ambrose Joseph Small was not born into wealth, it was created by him. Small entered this world on 11 January 1866 in Bradford, a small agricultural town in what is now Ontario. At about the time of his 12th birthday, Small's family relocated to Toronto, where his father managed the Walden Hotel. In a move typical of his time, he soon left school, and went to work at the hotel. As the years passed, young Small came to manage the hotel bar and began booking musical acts. The limited income derived from these jobs he supplemented with part-time work as an usher at the Grand Opera House (demolished in 1946), the premier establishment in Toronto. He became involved in various aspects of the venue and used its premises to operate a matchmaking service and work as a bookie taking bets on racehorses. In 1889, after an argument with the owner, he moved to the rival Toronto Opera House, where it is said he refined the talent that would bring him his riches.

Small was an irresponsible gambler, betting huge sums at the racetrack, and yet by 1892 he had begun buying interests in theatres in Toronto, Kingston, Peterborough, Hamilton and St Thomas.

As a businessman he was passionate, calculating and ruthless – the very same

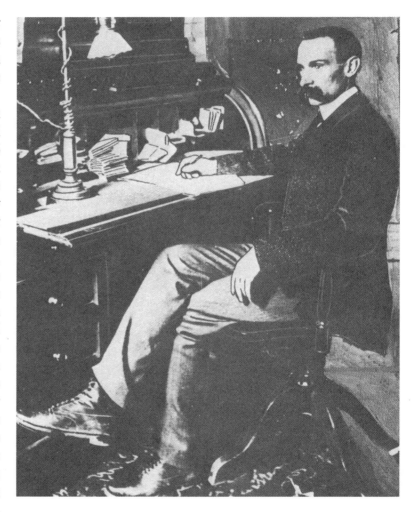

qualities that governed his romantic life. Small was handsome – if a bit on the short side – with fine tailored clothing and, of course, plenty of money. He was spotted frequently with one or another of the most beautiful young women in Toronto. Showgirls, who were more often than not employed in his own theatres, seemed to be amongst his favoured companions.

ABOVE:
**Ambrose Small at the desk where he made his fortune.**

And yet, as his 36th birthday approached, Small appeared to finally be focusing his attention on one woman. His stepmother's younger sister, Theresa Kormann was, perhaps, the most unconventional of choices. Where she was charitable, he was greedy. Theresa had a love of music and theatre, while her husband saw the performing arts only as a means of making money. She was a Catholic – and Small made no effort to hide his distaste for the faith. If the couple had anything in common, it was wealth; Theresa was the heiress to a brewing fortune.

They married and, with the help of his bride's inheritance, Small achieved one of his great goals: the purchase of the Grand Opera House, the venue at which he had once served as an usher. A secret room was built, complete with a well-stocked bar, a magnificent bed, and heavy drapes that would muffle the sound of his continuing dalliances with other women.

Success lay in the impresario's easy ability to adapt, moving from booking touring theatrical companies to vaudeville without so much as a hiccup. In the years leading up to the Great War, his empire expanded even more rapidly. Small came to own theatres throughout Ontario, and controlled bookings in 62 others, making him the

**RIGHT:**
**Theresa Kormann Small, a 'paragon of virtue' who was married to a womanizer.**

most powerful and wealthy man in the Canadian entertainment industry.

He had amassed a fortune, which he was determined to keep for himself. Unlike his wife, Small gave nothing to charity, nor would he volunteer or lend his name to any worthy cause. The poor he held in disdain.

His empire now secure in its dominance, with little opportunity for further growth, Small began to lose interest in it. With increasing frequency, the wealthy impresario passed his business dealings to his private secretary, John Doughty. It appeared that the years of great activity and growth had taxed Small. By the age of 50, his good looks had gone, as had his once abundant energy. Even his womanizing had been affected. Though he still was not faithful, his attentions were pretty much limited to one mistress, a woman named Clara Smith.

In November 1919, Small and his wife agreed to sell their business to Trans-Canada Theatres Ltd. for $1.7 million dollars. The couple would receive one million dollars on account, with the remaining funds to be paid in annual increments over a period of five years.

On the morning of 2 December, the day after the deal was finalized, Small purchased jewellery, a fur coat and a Cadillac for the long-suffering wife who had helped him become so very wealthy. That afternoon, he met briefly with his lawyer, E. W. M. Flock, at the Grand Opera House. As supper hour approached, Small left the building, stepping into a blinding snowstorm. He made his way to the corner of Yonge and Adelaide, where he stopped at a newsstand operated by Ralph Savein. Upon being told that the papers he requested had been held up by the storm, Small cursed and continued along his way. Savein watched his disappointed customer vanish into the falling December snow, never to be seen again.

Theresa waited several days before she reported her husband missing. All too aware of his extra-marital activities, her assumption had been that Small was

LEFT:
The Small house at 51 Glen Road in Toronto. It was here that Theresa spent her final years in semi-seclusion.

RIGHT:
**John Doughty, aka
Charles B. Cooper,
Small's private
secretary.**

with a woman. Once the impresario's disappearance became official, the greatest manhunt in Canadian history was begun. The participants were not limited to the authorities, but included a significant number of the public, no doubt spurred on by Theresa's offer of a $50,000 reward for information on her husband.

However, Ambrose Small was not the only person being sought by the police.

## Once the impresario's disappearance became official, the greatest manhunt in Canadian history was begun.

That same day, John Doughty had also disappeared. As it turned out, Doughty had resented losing his position as Small's personal secretary and had left town with $100,000 in negotiable Victory bonds he'd stolen from his former employer's safety deposit box at the Dominion Bank. The wanted man eventually reached Portland, Oregon, where he was arrested while working at a paper mill as Charles B. Cooper. Doughty was to spend five years in prison for his crime, during which time he had plenty of time to contemplate his bad judgement. Although it was true that he had lost his job as personal secretary, Small had arranged for

Trans-Canada Theatres Ltd. to take him on at a much higher salary.

Hundreds of leads were given to the police concerning Small, most seeming to indicate that the missing man had been murdered. One man reported that he'd witnessed Small being forced into a car on 2 December, not long after he'd left the newsstand. Another said that he'd seen four men burying an object the size of a man in a ravine close to Small's home. A woman insisted that several days before the disappearance had been made public she had seen a notice posted on a wall in the local convent which requested 'prayers for the repose of the soul of Ambrose J. Small'.

The waters off Toronto were dredged, the basement of the Small mansion was excavated and portions of the Grand Opera House were ripped up in the search, but the missing man was nowhere to be found.

After the search had entered its seventh year, desperate authorities brought in a Vienna psychic named Dr Maximilian Langsner to find Small. Sitting in his luxurious Toronto hotel suite, the doctor conducted séances and 'astral trips'. Police were dispatched, following each and every divination, but to no avail. The failure, Langsner maintained, had nothing to do with him; rather, the fault lay with the police themselves who were obscuring his visions.

For years after Small's disappearance theories and speculation dominated the press. Theresa's own belief was that her husband had been murdered by a former mistress. She revealed that she'd known of her husband's affairs, but had ignored them for much of their marriage. It wasn't until 1918 that she'd finally confronted her husband, after having discovered a collection of obscene letters written by Clara Smith. Small had destroyed the correspondence, promising to remain faithful from that point forward. However, unbeknownst to Theresa, her

LEFT:
Small's sisters, Mary and Gertrude, who fought so hard to keep their brother's fortune from his widow and the Catholic Church.

husband had continued seeing Clara, and had, in fact, had dinner with her on the day before his disappearance.

The public airing of private indiscretions stirred up a fight between Theresa and Small's sisters, Mary and Gertrude. Through the press, the pair worked hard to restore the reputation of their 'intelligent, hard-working' brother. He was, they declared, a man who had shunned debauchery and 'never showed the smallest tendency to deviate from the path of righteousness'. When their brother was pronounced officially dead in 1923, Mary and Gertrude went after his money, challenging a will that left everything to Theresa. Despite their efforts, it was determined that the entire estate, valued at $1,087,831.70, should go to the widow.

Theresa spent the remainder of her life in semi-seclusion. Upon her death, in 1935, the Small fortune went to the Catholic Church – the very institution that her husband had so despised.

As the remains of Ambrose Small have never been found, it cannot be said with absolute certainty that he did not read about his wife's bequest. Indeed, there were plenty of purported sightings of Small in the decades following his disappearance. He was spotted with two women on a Paris street. It was said that Small was living in a hotel he had bought in some unidentified South American country. Harry Blackstone, Sr., otherwise known as Blackstone the Magician, announced from the stage of Small's Grand Theatre in London, Ontario, that he had seen the former theatre magnate gambling in a Mexican casino.

## When their brother was pronounced officially dead in 1923, Mary and Gertrude went after his money, challenging a will that left everything to Theresa.

In his memoir, *When I Was Young*, the actor Raymond Massey briefly mentions that the charred remains of Small's body were found in the furnace of the Grand Theatre in London, Ontario. Is it possible that the actor was mistaken, or could it be that Massey, the son of a wealthy and powerful Toronto family, brother of Governor General Vincent Massey, was privy to information not shared with the general public?

The Toronto Police Department did not close their file on Ambrose Small until 1960, over 40 years after his disappearance. If still alive, perhaps enjoying a drink on a terrace in Montparnasse, he would have then been 94 years of age.

## THE GHOST OF AMBROSE SMALL

Even if Ambrose Small arranged his own disappearance, it is safe to say that, 14 decades after his birth, he is now amongst the deceased. His spirit is said to haunt London's Grand Theatre, a once beautiful building that Small had built in 1901, after the original burned to the ground.

The Grand serves as the setting for one of the more unlikely claims concerning Small's disappearance. A caretaker who worked at the theatre reported that he had once smelled burning flesh emanating from the furnace; convincing evidence, he argued, that Theresa and her previously unknown lover had killed and incinerated the impresario.

The earliest sighting of a ghost was made by Canadian comedienne Beatrice Lillie, who said that she saw a spirit motion towards her during a 1927 performance. Two years later, she returned to the Grand in Noel Coward's *This Year of Grace*. The story goes that while singing *Britannia Rules the Waves* the vaudevillian mistakenly repeated the second verse. The error delayed the entry of other cast members just long enough for them to narrowly avoid being hit by an arc light that fell from an overhead gantry: it landed on the stage just where they would have been standing.

Did Small's ghost cause the light to fall, or did he somehow influence Lillie to repeat herself? The answer to the question seems to be linked to how one views Small.

Other, more minor mishaps, have been blamed upon the impresario's ghost. Given his womanizing, it is perhaps predictable that many involve female actors and what we've come to call a 'wardrobe malfunction'.

More often than not, sightings at the Grand focus on the Smalls' box, which was said to feature a secret passageway leading to the female stars' dressing room. However, not all of the ghost's appearances have been in the box or on the stage. In 1956, Charmion King, who was one of Canada's leading actresses, is said to have seen a mysterious man standing at the foot of the theatre's stairway. She later identified the figure as Small, after viewing a photograph of the missing impresario. The following year a ghostly figure was spotted offstage as it ascended a ladder.

Séances conducted on the Grand's stage in the mid 1970s indicated that a solution to Small's disappearance was located within the theatre's west wall. Unfortunately, this side of the building has been the only one left untouched in subsequent renovations and so the chance to explore it has not yet arisen.

ABOVE RIGHT:
The stage at Small's Grand Theatre in London, Ontario.

# The Strange Case of Brother XII

The west coast of North America seems to hold some attraction for cult leaders. It was in California that West Virginian Charles Manson founded his notorious 'family'. Jim Jones' People's Temple flourished in San Francisco, before moving to Guyana. Further north in Canada, various islands off the coast of British Columbia served as home for the Aquarian Foundation, described as, 'the fastest growing religious movement of the early 20th century'. Those less polite would describe the Aquarian Foundation as a cult, lead by a charlatan named Brother XII.

Of course, Brother XII was not the cult leader's legal name; he had been born Edward Arthur Wilson, on 25 July 1878 in Birmingham, England. His parents were devoted followers of Edward Irving, an early 19th-century clergyman who had prophesized the imminent return of Christ. As a child, Wilson had contact with supernatural beings he had then thought were angels – or so the mystic claimed. He also asserted that he was not the son of an Englishwoman, but that he had been born to an Indian princess.

Though many of Wilson's claims concerning his background have been discounted, a few of his more modest stories have basis in fact. For example, he told the truth when writing that he had trained on a Royal Navy windjammer – though his claim that he used these skills in trafficking African slaves is almost certainly a fabrication.

Given his marketable skills as a sailor, it is likely that Wilson travelled extensively. His first known contact with Canada occurred in 1905, when he was living in Victoria. Though a manual labourer – for a time he'd been employed as a baggage handler for the Dominion Express Company – Wilson was anything but a robust individual.

ABOVE:
**An illustration after the only photographic image of Edward Arthur Wilson, the mysterious Brother XII.**

However, lack of physical strength appeared to have no effect on his abilities; he spent much of his free time sailing the Gulf of Georgia and the Strait of Juan de Fuca.

Wilson never stayed in one place for very long. While it might be that he was on something of a spiritual quest, he was known to have left a trail of personal debt in his wake. When leaving the Victoria rooming house he had called home, Wilson promised his landlady he would one day return, 'as the head of a new religion' and pay his bill in full.

In 1912, Wilson arrived in San Diego, where he joined Madame Blavatsky's Theosophical Society. He seemed to move from place to place within California, before leaving the United States for Tahiti. If Wilson is to be believed, his whereabouts and rather unfocused quest for spiritual truth become clear on 22 October 1924. It

ABOVE:
**Elena Petrovna Gan, better known as Madame Blavatsky, the founder of Theosophy.**

was on that day, while visiting the south of France, that he heard the 'unutterable majesty and power' of a being he called 'the Voice'. According to Wilson, in, 'faint but very clear and wonderfully sweet' words, he was told:

*Thôu who hast worn the double crown of upper and lower Egypt, of the high knowledge and the low, humble thyself. Prepare thy heart, for the mighty ones have need of thee. Thou shalt rebuild, thou shalt restore. Therefore, prepare thy mind for that which shall illumine thee.*

Thus, Wilson had been made aware that he was a pharaoh, charged with reclaiming the truths of ancient Egypt. Henceforth a disciple of 'the Voice', one of the twelve 'Masters of the Great White Lodge', Wilson adopted the name Brother XII. Writing in trance, he set down the teachings of his master; documents upon which a spiritual movement would be established. A little over two years later, he returned to Vancouver Island, intent on building a community that would be 'THE center of spiritual energy and knowledge for the whole continent of North America – for the whole world in the not distant future.' In Brother XII's grand design there were to have been two other 'centers' – in California and Mexico – but the one in British Columbia, at Cedar-by-the-Sea, ten kilometres (5 miles) outside Nanaimo, would be the primary place from which would evolve an advanced 'sixth sub-race' of people who would build a new civilization after the coming Armageddon.

The first general meeting of this body of believers, which he called the Aquarian Foundation, was held on 25 July 1927, his 49th birthday. There was reason to celebrate; Brother XII was heading the fastest-growing spiritual movement on the continent.

However, the adulation of his followers was not enough. Brother XII sought to extend his reach into the political arena. He looked south of the border, meeting with senators, congressmen and the Ku Klux Klan in an effort to establish the 'Third Party'. Racist Alabama senator James Thomas Heflin was recruited to run for Brother XII's Third Party against Republican candidate Herbert Hoover and Alfred Smith, who was running for the Democratic Party. 'Elect Hoover, and you will be plundered in a thousand ways', warned Brother XII. 'Elect Smith, and freedom will become only a memory in the land.' In July 1928, three months shy of that year's presidential election, Brother XII was so bold as to declare: 'I expect to select and will select the man who will be the next president of the United States.'

## The adulation of his followers was not enough. Brother XII sought to extend his reach into the political arena.

A great amount of money – most of it American – flowed into Brother XII's colony. Socialite Mary Wortham Thomas Connally, whose family had arrived in the New World on the *Mayflower*, donated $25,000 at the end of a three-hour meeting with Brother XII at Toronto's King Edward Hotel. Brother XII made a point of depositing the money in his personal bank account. Untold thousands were given by Roger Painter, the 'Poultry King of Florida'; including $90,000 in cash offered during a 1929 visit to Cedar-by-the-Sea. Those who had chosen to live at the colony were expected to sever all ties with their former lives in the outside world. All that they had possessed was expected to have been converted into gold coins, which they would surrender when moving to

Cedar-by-the-Sea. Brother XII then placed these offerings in sealed mason jars: he explained the necessity of this latter sacrifice in a personal letter:

*True discipleship means a life dedicated to the service of humanity, it is diametrically opposed to the preferences of the personal self. No compromise between these two is possible. Therefore, the first requirement is THE SURRENDER OF PERSONAL POSSESSIONS, an actual not a theoretical surrender. If the disciple is truly dedicated, it follows that all he has is included in the dedication of himself. This is the first requirement and it constitutes at once a safeguard and a test which the insecure will be unable to face.*

Not all attempts to better the Aquarian Foundation involved the surrender of wealth. Though a married woman, New Yorker Myrtle Wells Baumgartner shared Brother XII's bed. In what was claimed as an attempt to provide the spiritual leader with a successor, she twice became pregnant.

## Those who had chosen to live at the colony were expected to sever all ties with their former lives in the outside world.

Both terms ended in miscarriage, but this did not shake Mrs Baumgartner's belief that she and Brother XII had been lovers in ancient Egypt. When confronted by his wife, and other followers who questioned the relationship, Brother XII declared that it had nothing to do with self-gratification; rather, it was a case of 'self-immolation on the part of those who would give their bodies to be burned that we may bear witness to the Truth.'

In November 1928, Herbert Hoover won an easy victory over Albert Smith; Third Party candidate James Thomas Heflin failed to win a single electoral vote. Little more than a year after it had begun, Brother XII's utopian colony had been exposed as something less than perfect. After her second miscarriage, Myrtle Baumgartner had suffered a nervous breakdown. The governors of the Aquarian Foundation had come to question his authority and petitioned the province to revoke the society's charter. Robert England, the secretary-treasurer, wrote that, 'The Brother XII is no longer working in or through the body and faculties of Edward A. Wilson'.

In the face of this revolt, Brother XII successfully sought another donation from Mary Connally, with which he purchased even more property, forming a new community called the Brothers' Center.

This new colony, centred on DeCourcy Island, was a place for true disciples dedicated to the service of humanity. It was overseen by Mabel Skottowe, known to all as Madame Z. A forceful, sinister Englishwoman, she became Brother XII's eyes, ears and his partner in bed. They married – not legally, of course – in some sort of contrived ritual created by the groom.

The newlyweds spent much of 1930 in England, nearly 10,000 kilometres (6,000 miles) away from the Brothers' Center. After their return, things changed dramatically at the colony. Mary Connally, the now-impoverished *Mayflower* socialite, was made to chop wood, scrub floors and plough fields. Other disciples were treated in a similar manner – all in an effort to strengthen

TOP:
A branch of the
Aquarian Foundation
in Seattle.

MAIN IMAGE: One of
the society's many
buildings, used as a
schoolhouse and later
as a women's
dormitory.

their souls and prove themselves worthy. Through their seemingly never-ending tasks, the disciples created a prosperous community in the midst of the Great Depression.

Despite past problems, the colony seemed to be on even keel. However, in early 1932 all was rocked when authorities began investigating complaints that had been made by a former disciple. After police and immigration officers visited one of Brother XII's islands, he began to stock up on firearms and ammunition. Fortifications were built, and warning shots were fired at fishing vessels that happened too close to the colony.

Brother XII's behaviour became increasingly erratic and cruel. He delighted in destruction, placed his disciples on rations, and forced them to maintain the fields around the clock. And yet, not one dared challenge him or his mistress for fear of losing their souls.

As the hardship continued and conditions within the colony worsened, speculation formed within the colony that Brother XII and Madam Z had gone insane. Isolated, cut off from the outside world, the disciples on DeCourcy Island gathered the courage to request a meeting with their increasingly reclusive leader. This, in turn, led to banishment, as those who dared question their work were transported by tugboat back to Cedar-by-the-Sea.

However, Brother XII had miscalculated; those who were banished regrouped, determined to continue without their leader. In an attempt to regain at least a portion of their former riches, some members went to court against the Brothers' Center. Roger Painter testified that Brother XII and Madame Z had tried using black magic to kill their enemies. The stories presented were simply too much to believe, and yet the plaintiffs were successful.

Ultimately, however, the sensational and embarrassing court case had been

LEFT:
**Socialite Mary Wortham Thomas Connally, who gave all her great wealth to Brother XII.**

in vain; Brother XII and Madame Z had fled, taking with them an estimated $400,000 in riches.

It is known that the couple returned to England, leaving by ocean liner from the Port of Montreal. They lived in Devonshire for a year or so before leaving for the Continent. It seemed that Brother XII's health was failing; he sought medical treatment in Switzerland from Dr Roger Schmidt, the man who had been his personal physician in Cedar-by-the-Sea.

On 7 November 1934, Edward Arthur Wilson – Brother XII – died at Neuchâtel. According to a death certificate signed by Schmidt, the 56-year-old reincarnation of Osiris – as he claimed – had fallen victim to angina pectoris. Brother XII left no property; his 'widow', Madame Z, simply vanished.

And so it seemed that Brother XII had

died, perhaps to be reincarnated. However, many former followers of the good brother found his demise suspicious. Simply put, the sudden death not only seemed convenient, but left behind a good question: what happened to the gold coins?

**Many former followers of the good brother found his demise suspicious. Simply put, the sudden death not only seemed convenient, but left behind a good question: what happened to the gold coins?**

Treasure hunters descended on the island, searching for the sealed mason jars. One dedicated treasure seeker, a former employee of Mary Connally, purportedly found a concrete vault buried on Valdes Island. He entered to find it empty, except for a roll of tarpaper upon which was written in Brother XII's hand: 'For fools and traitors, nothing!'

In all likelihood, Brother XII and Madame Z took the jars full of gold when they left the colony. Less than two years after Brother XII's death, Mary Connally is known to have dispatched the supposedly dead man's lawyer, Frank Cunliffe, to San Francisco. There, aboard an ocean liner docked in the harbour, he was given a briefcase full of cash by a man who matched Brother XII's description.

Then, in 1937, Cunliffe's son, Donald, was present when the lawyer received a trans-Atlantic telephone call from a man whom the operator identified as 'Mr Wilson'. The younger Cunliffe's belief that this Mr Wilson and Brother XII were one and the same was all but confirmed by his father, who remarked, 'I hope he goes to hell!'

## THE INVOCATION OF LIGHT

At precisely 5 am, on 27 April 1926, Brother XII claimed that he recovered an invocation that he said dated to the reign of pharaoh Akhenaten.

Called 'The Invocation of Light', followers were expected to repeat these words upon arising each morning and in the evenings before retiring to bed:

*O Thou Who bringest the Dawn,*
*Who renewest the Day without ceasing.*
*Whose splendour is the Brightness of the Morning;*
*Fountain of Life and Source of Light Eternal.*
*Increase in us Thy Knowledge and Thy Strength.*
*Thou Who shinest in the East.*
*Who showest the West Thy glory.*
*And art supreme in the high heaven;*
*Thou fillest Thy Houses with Light.*
*And Thy Mansions with hidden Power.*
*Thou sustainest the Seven Lords,*
*The Shining Ones Who keep Thy Path,*
*And we, who serve Thee through Their Ray.*
*O Light ineffable.*
*Increase in us Thy Wisdom and Thy Power.*
*Dwell in us, we are One in Thee.*

# CHAPTER 4:
# MYSTERIOUS DEATHS

# Tom Thomson on Canoe Lake

In the realm of Canadian art, Tom Thomson reigns supreme. The most influential of all Canadian artists, he held such sway over the painters who would one day form the Group of Seven that he is frequently misrepresented as having been one of their number; in fact, Thomson died three years before the formation came into being. As the centenary of his death approaches, the circumstances of his drowning continue to be the subject of speculation and rumour.

Thomson was born 5 August 1877, not far from the Ontario hamlet of Claremont. His early life was spent on the southwest shore of Georgian Bay, in the village of Leith, where his body now rests. As a young man he appeared restless, moving from an apprenticeship at a foundry, to volunteering to fight in the Second Boer War, to brief stints at business schools in Chatham, Ontario; and Seattle, Washington. A $2,000 inheritance from his grandfather seems to have been squandered. By 1907, he was working for Grip Limited, a Toronto design firm, where he became acquainted with several future members of the Group of Seven. Five years later, he began travelling throughout the untouched Canadian countryside, seeking inspiration for his landscape paintings.

Thomson struggled to become a full-time artist, living in squalor and taking on a variety of jobs, including one as a fire ranger in Algonquin Provincial

Park. He'd first visited the park in 1912, and since that time had returned whenever possible. In late March of 1917, Thomson returned for what would turn out to be his final stay. He took a room at Mowat Lodge, located on the shore of Canoe Lake. It was a modest establishment, one at which he had lodged on several previous visits to the park.

ABOVE:
An illustration by painter Andrew Hamilton depicting Tom Thomson by the shore of Canoe Lake, taken from a photograph dated c. 1916.

RIGHT:
**Canoe Lake, painted in the style of Tom Thomson. The body of water was one of his favourite subjects.**

Thomson was at the top of his artistic form when one dull, grey Sunday, 8 July 1917, he vanished into a light rain while canoeing on the lake. Although the canoe was later found upside down in the lake, searchers noted that the paddles had been strapped, and so held out hope that the artist was alive. Speculation that he might be stranded, perhaps on one of the many islands, came to an abrupt end eight days later when his body was pulled from the water.

The official cause of death, accidental drowning, has always been questioned. Those who knew him could not accept the judgement that a healthy outdoorsman – a 'modern *coureur de bois*' is how one friend described him – could meet such an end. Not yet 30 years of age, Thomson was an expert canoeist; it simply stretched the imagination that he might drown on a summer day in a lake known for its calm waters.

Suspicions were raised by the fact that the local coroner, Dr Arthur E. Ranney, had determined the official cause of death without performing an autopsy. Thomson's body had supposedly been in such an advanced state of decomposition that immediate burial was called for. Before he was laid to rest, Thomson's corpse had been examined, externally, by Dr G. W. Howland, a vacationing physician who just happened to be one of the people who had found the dead painter floating in Canoe Lake. The coroner relied on Howland's conclusion that Thomson had drowned, despite the fact that no water had been found in his lungs. It was also noted that he had a head wound, which could have happened after death. More sinister, perhaps, was the length of fishing line wrapped 17 times around one of his legs.

Within days, Thomson's elder brother George moved to have the body exhumed and buried in the family plot beside the Presbyterian church at Leith. This began with a grizzly disinterment, conducted in the dead of night, in which Thomson's fine oak casket was dug up and his body transferred to a second casket. The supposedly empty coffin was then placed back in the grave and covered over. This operation, performed single-handedly by a local undertaker, Franklin W. Churchill, has been viewed with suspicion. There has been considerable speculation that Thomson's body was never removed from his Canoe Lake grave, and that what was later sent by rail to Leith was nothing but a weighted coffin. As there was no witness to the nocturnal exhumation, and as Churchill had Thomson's steel casket soldered shut, it would have been possible for some sleight of hand to have come into play.

Thomson's friend and proprietor of Mowat Lodge, Shannon Fraser, recounted that he'd dropped off the undertaker at the burial site and had returned three hours later to find the task had been completed. In uncovering the casket, hoisting it out of the ground, transferring the body and then refilling the grave, it appeared that Churchill had not even broken into a sweat. In his account, Fraser added that the casket appeared to him surprisingly light.

One rumour has it that Thomson's friends, in the belief that they were following the dead man's wishes, moved his body to a second grave overlooking Canoe Lake before Churchill arrived.

In 1956, nearly four decades after the painter's death, William Little and some friends travelled to Canoe Lake, where they searched for the grave. They uncovered a casket and corpse that bore every indication as belonging to Thomson. For a time, it appeared that the mystery as to cause of death had been solved: the corpse's skull contained a hole in the temple region. However, those claiming conspiracy were later disappointed when forensic examinations determined that the body was that of a First Nations man. The finding did not dissuade Little, who continued to maintain that he and his friends had indeed found the body of Tom Thomson.

For their part, the Thomson family has been resolute in its determination that the gravesite in Leith remains undisturbed.

William Little is at the forefront of those who believe that Thomson's death is related to a supposed love affair with a young woman named Winnifred Trainor. Winnie, as she was known, lived with her family in a cabin on the shore of Canoe Lake. Evidence that indicates that she was at the very least a friend of Thomson is joined by rumour that she was pregnant with his child. Some have suggested that she had been pressuring Thomson into marriage, scheduled to take place in the autumn, and that the painter chose suicide in place of the altar.

A less titillating, more straight-forward theory points to the well-known animosity shared between Thomson and Martin Blecher, Jr, who spent summers at a cottage he owned on the lake. A German-American, Blecher had argued frequently with Thomson over the ongoing First World War. Indeed, he had done so on the evening before the painter's disappearance. It is not difficult to imagine that the mutual dislike might have at some point broken out into violence. If so, might it be that Blecher killed Thomson, and then disposed of the body in the lake? This theory would account for the absence of water in the dead painter's lungs – it might also explain why it was Blecher who found Thomson's abandoned, upside-down canoe.

## Might it be that Blecher killed Thomson, and then disposed of the body in the lake?

The idea that Thomson might have died, whether intentionally or inadvertently, at the hands of Blecher, is not dissimilar to a 1973 account given by a woman named Daphne Crombie. According to Crombie, who spent much of the early part of 1917 at Canoe Lake, the painter was killed in an alcohol-fuelled argument with Shannon Fraser. It seems that the lodge owner had borrowed money to purchase canoes and had been tardy with repayment. At some point, Fraser struck his friend,

ABOVE:
**Tom Thomson's cabin and winter studio, now in the McMichael Conservation Collection in Kleinberg, Ontario.**

who fell to the floor, hitting his head on a fire grate. Fraser then placed Thomson in his canoe, towed it out on the lake, and capsized it.

Daphne Crombie witnessed none of these events; rather, she was told of them by Annie, Shannon Fraser's wife, who had been awoken at night to help dispose of the body. Herein lies a problem: Crombie places the murder as having taken place in the small hours of 8 July, while park ranger Mark Robinson, a friend of Thomson, says that he saw the painter paddling his canoe in the early afternoon of the same day. Those who believe Crombie's story to be a reflection of true events point out that Robinson only saw Thomson – and even then it was from a great distance, leaving the possibility that the park ranger could have been mistaken.

Thomson's friendship with Robinson raises another proposed scenario, in which the painter stumbled upon a group of poachers and was murdered to keep him silent.

Might Thomson have died in a more mundane fashion? It may be that he was pulled into the water after suddenly snagging a large lake trout, or perhaps he just lost his balance while urinating over the side of his canoe. But it is somehow unacceptable to think that the life of so talented and vibrant an individual could end in such a manner.

All those who lived on Canoe Lake during Tom Thomson's fatal summer are now long dead. Unless some form of written confession is uncovered, it is unlikely that the mystery of his death will ever be solved. It is, perhaps, time to turn our attentions way from his death and toward his corpus. The greatest unknown in Thomson's story is what artistic heights he could have reached had he returned from that final canoe trip.

# THE TOM THOMSON MEMORIAL CAIRN

**Thomson's friend, J. E. H. Macdonald, designed a brass inscription that was placed on a memorial cairn at Hayhurst Point, Canoe Lake, on 30 September 1917.**

TO THE MEMORY OF
TOM THOMSON
ARTIST, WOODSMAN
AND GUIDE
WHO WAS DROWNED IN CANOE LAKE
JULY 8TH, 1917
HE LIVED HUMBLY BUT PASSIONATELY
WITH THE WILD IT MADE HIM BROTHER
TO ALL UNTAMED THINGS OF NATURE
IT DREW HIM APART AND REVEALED
ITSELF WONDERFULLY TO HIM
IT SENT HIM OUT FROM THE WOODS
ONLY TO SHOW THESE REVELATIONS
THROUGH HIS ART AND IT TOOK
HIM TO ITSELF AT LAST.

HIS FELLOW ARTISTS AND OTHER FRIENDS AND ADMIRERS
JOIN GLADLY IN THIS TRIBUTE TO
HIS CHARACTER AND GENIUS
HIS BODY IS BURIED AT
OWEN SOUND ONTARIO NEAR
WHERE HE WAS BORN
AUGUST
1877

# Harry Houdini's Final Curtain

RIGHT:
**Ehrich Weiss, better known as Harry Houdini, the greatest escape artist of all time.**

Each Halloween, the anniversary of Harry Houdini's death, people around the world gather at tables and hold séances hoping against hope to contact the great escape artist. For ten years after his death, his widow, Bess, held annual séances, but her husband never appeared. After her last attempt, on the roof of the Knickerbocker Hotel in downtown Los Angeles, Mrs Houdini extinguished the flame that she had kept burning beside a photograph of her husband since his death. As she later said, 'Ten years is long enough to wait for any man.' It was left to others to carry on the effort.

The tradition is an odd one in that Houdini had spent much of his career debunking spiritualists. It has been said that Houdini's training as a magician allowed him to expose those who had been successful in deceiving scientists and academics. He was perhaps the most valuable member of a five-person committee that offered a substantial prize to anyone who could demonstrate supernatural abilities. The prize was never collected.

Among those whom he discredited was the celebrated Canadian-born Boston medium Mina 'Margery' Crandon who, Houdini asserted, had been altered by her surgeon husband so that she might conceal a 'teleplasmatic' hand. Houdini chronicled the debunking of Mrs Crandon and others in his pamphlet, *Houdini Exposes the Tricks Used by Boston Medium 'Margery'* and the books *Margery the Medium* and *A Magician Among the Spirits*.

The latter publication was two years old when Houdini embarked on a tour that would take him to McGill University in Montreal. His appearance on 19 October, at what was then Canada's most respected institution of higher learning, was not without controversy. Then a student of 16, the accomplished Canadian poet and pornographer John Glassco described Houdini as having presented a, 'vaudeville lecture on spiritualism'. F. R. Scott, who would one day become the university's Dean of the Faculty of Law,

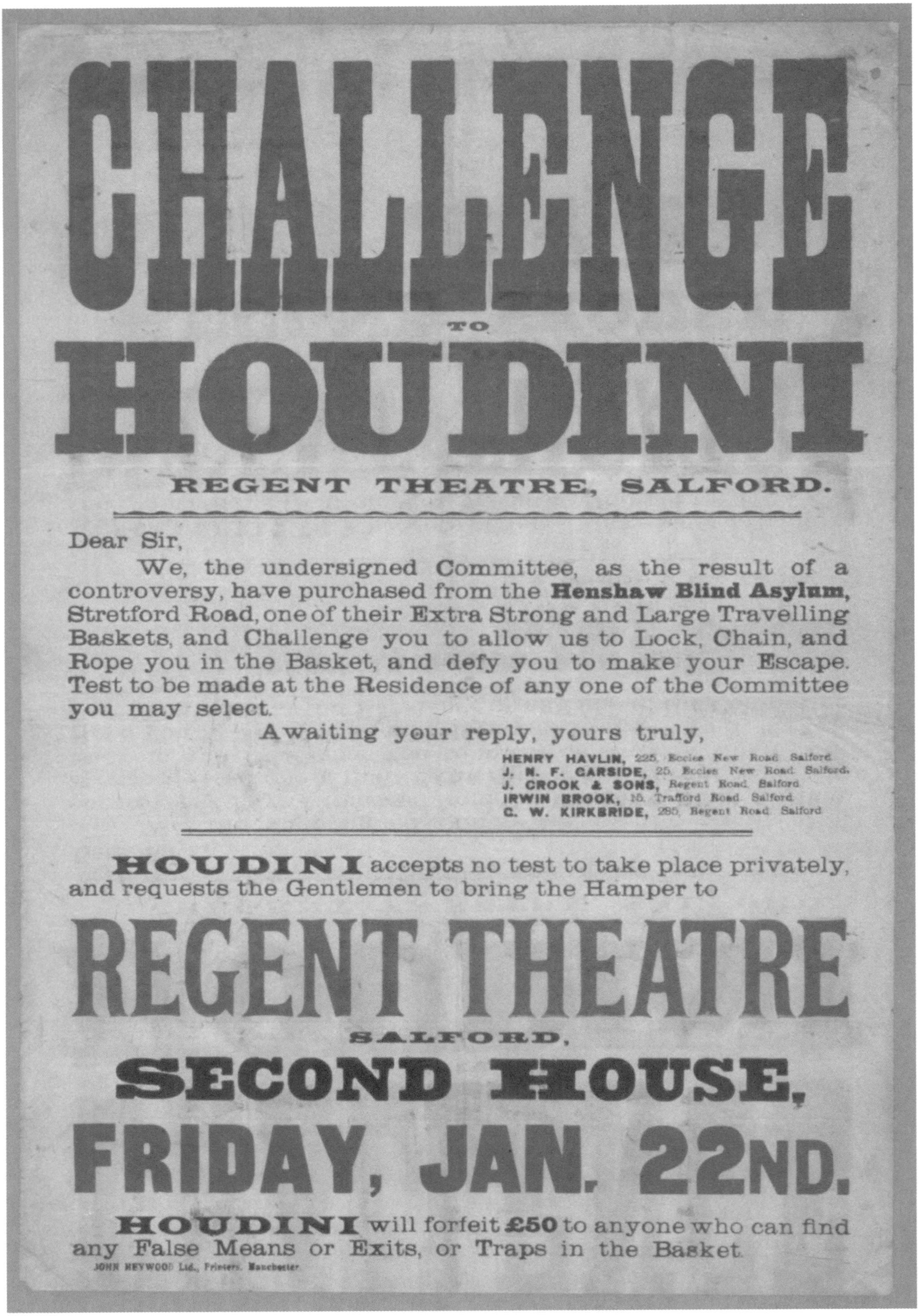

# CHALLENGE

## TO

# HOUDINI

### REGENT THEATRE, SALFORD.

Dear Sir,

We, the undersigned Committee, as the result of a controversy, have purchased from the **Henshaw Blind Asylum**, Stretford Road, one of their Extra Strong and Large Travelling Baskets, and Challenge you to allow us to Lock, Chain, and Rope you in the Basket, and defy you to make your Escape. Test to be made at the Residence of any one of the Committee you may select.

Awaiting your reply, yours truly,

**HENRY HAVLIN**, 225, Eccles New Road Salford.
**J. N. F. GARSIDE**, 25, Eccles New Road Salford.
**J. CROOK & SONS**, Regent Road Salford
**IRWIN BROOK**, 15, Trafford Road, Salford
**C. W. KIRKBRIDE**, 285, Regent Road Salford

---

**HOUDINI** accepts no test to take place privately, and requests the Gentlemen to bring the Hamper to

# REGENT THEATRE

### SALFORD,

# SECOND HOUSE,

# FRIDAY, JAN. 22ND.

**HOUDINI** will forfeit £50 to anyone who can find any False Means or Exits, or Traps in the Basket.

JOHN HEYWOOD Ltd., Printers, Manchester.

submitted a poem that was published anonymously in the *McGill Fortnightly Review*:

> *Masses heard the great Houdini,*
> *Masses shouted for the Queenie,*
> *Did you ever see such asses*
> *As the educated masses!*

When published, talk of the 'Queenie' – a reference to a recent visit by Queen Marie of Romania – was little more than background noise; the campus of McGill was abuzz with talk that a student, J. Gordon Whitehead, had killed the world's greatest showman.

On 22 October, three days after his lecture delivered at the invitation of Dr William Tait, a professor of psychology, Houdini had been scheduled to perform the sixth of eight shows at the Princess Theatre on St Catherine Street. He'd arrived at the venue that morning and, relaxing in his dressing room, received Whitehead and two other students, Jacques Price and Samuel Smilovitz. At

## The idea that the great escapologist could be killed by two or three punches delivered by a mere college boy did not sit well with some.

some point Whitehead punched Houdini several times in the stomach.

Houdini left Montreal by train, travelling to his next engagement in Detroit. He'd sought medical treatment upon his arrival, and was diagnosed with acute appendicitis. Still, he insisted upon performing, famously collapsing on the stage of the Garrick Theatre. The following morning he was rushed to hospital, where he underwent an emergency appendicectomy. Despite his best efforts, Houdini's surgeon, Dr Charles Kennedy, expected the showman to live no more than twelve hours. And yet, Houdini remained alive, fighting for his life,

for a full seven days following the operation. The patient appeared to be making good progress when he took a sudden turn for the worse. On the afternoon of 31 October 1926, Houdini died of peritonitis brought on by a ruptured appendix.

Kennedy believed that Houdini's appendix had ruptured on 24 October, likely as the train had passed somewhere in the vicinity of St Thomas, Ontario. Mysteriously, Houdini's final letter, dictated the day before his death, was addressed 'My dear Thomas'. The recipient was never identified and the letter was never sent.

Houdini's fatal failure, it seems, was in not seeking help before arriving in Detroit. Indeed, there is a great deal of evidence suggesting that the escape artist was suffering from appendicitis well before Montreal.

As the beneficiary of her husband's estate, it was in Bess Houdini's interest that the death be deemed accidental – doing so would double the amount of a $25,000 life insurance policy. Though her lawyers made inquiries about the incident, they determined that the showman's death was not the result of the student's actions; rather, that Houdini had died of natural causes.

That Mrs Houdini's lawyers arrived at their conclusion is interesting: in the early part of the 20th century it was thought that, though improbable, appendicitis could be provoked through a blow to the stomach. Indeed, the escape artist's widow received the additional payment after the physicians who treated Houdini concluded that there was a direct connection between the blows received in Montreal and the death by peritonitis. Modern medical opinion, however, sides with the lawyers: it is simply impossible for blunt trauma, such as the punches delivered by Whitehead, to cause appendicitis.

The clearest picture we have as to what actually transpired in the dressing room of the Princess Theatre comes through the investigation that was

LEFT:
**A publicity poster for a 1909 performance by Houdini at the Regent Theatre in Salford, England.**

undertaken by New York Life Insurance. In statements gathered, members of Houdini's entourage agreed that the performer had been in excellent shape prior to the blows received on the morning of 22 October 1926. None of these employees witnessed the violence that took place within the dressing room – for this we must rely on affidavits provided by J. Gordon Whitehead, Samuel Smilovitz and Jacques Price.

According to the documents, after having seen a drawing Smilovitz had made at the McGill lecture, Houdini had invited the artist to sketch his portrait as he relaxed in the dressing room. Smilovitz had brought Jacques Price, an acquaintance, to meet the famous performer. They had been there some time when, at approximately 10.45 am, Whitehead was admitted to the dressing room. There followed some casual conversation, with the topic turning to Houdini's strength and mental acuteness.

According to Smilovitz and Price, Whitehead seemed focussed in the former. Both men stated that Whitehead had asked Houdini whether it was true that he was impervious to punches in the stomach. Here, the assailant's statements are at variance with the other witnesses': Whitehead claims that he was invited by Houdini to punch him in the stomach. Though the testimony is vague, it would appear that Houdini received between three and five blows in total, after which the four men resumed their conversation.

After Smilovitz completed his sketch, the three men left. Whitehead added that he visited Houdini on two subsequent occasions and noted something that was not observed by Smilovitz and Price: 'Houdini gave me the impression of being a very sick man but his determination to keep going was equally apparent.' Why Whitehead felt he should challenge, then strike, 'a very sick man', he left unexplained.

Whitehead goes on to say that he 'struck Houdini quite moderately', that the showman smiled, laughed and told the student to hit him again. Smilovitz and Price, on the other hand, claim that Whitehead laid 'very heavy hammer-like blows below the belt'. In their accounts there is no smile, no laughter and no request for a second punch.

The idea that the great escapologist could be killed by two or three punches delivered by a mere college boy did not

## Both men stated that Whitehead had asked Houdini whether it was true that he was impervious to punches in the stomach.

sit well with some. There was talk of conspiracy – someone must have been out to get the Great Houdini.

More than one pair of eyes fell on Mina 'Margery' Crandon, the 'Witch of Beacon Hill', who had in December 1924 predicted that Houdini would be dead in less than a year. His book *Margery the Medium* quotes Mrs Crandon as threatening: 'Houdini, if you misrepresent me from the stage of the Keith's [a Boston theatre], some of my friends will come and give you a good beating.' This raised the question: were Whitehead's punches the 'good beating'? Moreover, were other 'friends' involved?

Gordon Nelles, a student reporter with the *McGill Daily*, recalled meeting Houdini four days before Whitehead delivered his blows. At that time, the showman told him that he had received a punch to the stomach that he hadn't prepared for.

Several witnesses saw another student, usually identified as Gerald Pickleman, sucker punch Houdini at an informal demonstration after his McGill lecture. Honoré Larin, night clerk of Montreal's Prince of Wales Hotel, at which Houdini had stayed, said that he had seen the guest punched as he was reading a newspaper in the lobby.

Might it be that several people were hired to deliver to Houdini the beating that Mrs Crandon felt he deserved?

Those who cry 'conspiracy' point to the beginning of the month in which Houdini died, when his wife became ill with ptomaine poisoning.

In conversation and correspondence, Houdini himself had stated that the bogus spiritualists were looking to do him harm. He told novelist Fulton Oursler, 'Probably I'm talking to you for the last time; they are going to kill me.'

When Oursler asked who, the escapologist responded, 'Fraudulent spirit mediums.'

It seems that the showman's fate was predicted by at least one person on the other side of the Atlantic, Jean Conan Doyle, the wife of Sir Arthur Conan Doyle. The popular writer and the showman had once been friends, but had experienced a very public falling out over the validity of spiritualism. A firm believer, Doyle became troubled by Houdini's persistent efforts to discredit

BELOW:
**Medium Mina 'Margery' Crandon, considered by some conspiracy theorists to be the force behind Houdini's untimely death.**

the high-profile mediums of the day. The writer's belief was such that he became convinced that Houdini possessed paranormal abilities, which enabled the showman to pull off his stunts. Doyle was certain that his former friend's powers were so great that he was able to impede others blessed with similar faculties.

Shortly after the escapologist's death, Doyle did not hesitate in announcing to the world that his wife, 'under spirit influence', had written: 'Houdini is Doomed, Doomed, Doomed!' seven months earlier.

LEFT:
A firm believer in the paranormal, Sir Arthur Conan Doyle praised Mina 'Margery' Crandon in his 1926 book *The History of Spiritualism.*

## WHO WAS J. GORDON WHITEHEAD?

J. Gordon Whitehead told Houdini that he was a divinity student at McGill, yet the university's Faculty of Theology has no record of his enrolment. More than one biography of Houdini claims that Whitehead went on to serve as a clergyman in the United States. It has even been suggested by those who have no knowledge of Houdini's debunking of spiritualism that Whitehead had intentionally killed the showman because he had popularized mysticism. Other sources describe Whitehead as an architecture student and a 'college boxer'. In his affidavit, Whitehead stated that he was working at 'the library of McGill University' – and yet the institution holds no record of his employment.

Jocelyn Gordon Whitehead, the person recognized by Houdini's insurers as having delivered the fatal blows, was born 25 November 1895 at Gourack, Scotland. By 1914, he was living in British Columbia, where he graduated from Kelowna High School. He did, indeed, attend McGill – enrolling at the rather advanced age of 30 – but dropped out shortly after his visit to Houdini. Whitehead died of malnutrition at the Queen Elizabeth Hospital on Marlowe Street in Montreal on 5 July 1954. He was alone and left no heirs.

ABOVE LEFT:
McGill University, alleged alma mater of J. Gordon Whitehead.

# The Murder of Sir Harry Oakes

ABOVE:
**Sir Harry Oakes, the wealthiest man in Canada – though he rarely dressed the part.**

**M**urder amongst the wealthy was once a staple of detective fiction. Agatha Christie, Dorothy L. Sayers and Sir Arthur Conan Doyle used the country manor as a setting of untimely deaths from unnatural causes. Other writers, of less talent and imagination, have relied on countless stereotypical dark and stormy nights in setting up their mystery stories. In the summer of 1943, these elements came together in the bedroom of a Bahamas mansion with the brutal murder of Sir Harry Oakes, Canada's wealthiest man.

Oakes did not begin life as a Canadian. He was born two days before Christmas,

1874, in Sangerville, Maine, a town of less than 1,000, some 150 kilometres (100 miles) west of the border with Quebec. His family was one of the oldest and most prominent in the area. He was educated at the finest schools in Maine: Foxcroft Academy and Bowdoin College, before leaving for New York State to attend Syracuse Medical School. It was not a happy time. Oakes found the discipline difficult. Moreover, his discovery, rather late in his studies, that the average salary of a medical doctor then amounted to roughly $3,000 per annum, discouraged him. His dreams of great wealth were seemingly at odds with his chosen profession. Oakes cared little for the health and wellbeing of others – it was wealth that he sought. Increasingly, the young man's thoughts focused on the easier riches lying beneath the soil, and in the summer of 1896, after two years of comfortable, if unadventurous life as a medical student, Oakes set out to join the Klondike Gold Rush. Supported by his family, he arrived in the Yukon after the frenzy had reached its climax. However, he did make good money through his medical training by treating victims of frostbite.

Other adventures followed: Oakes was shipwrecked off the coast of Alaska, captured by Russian sailors (or so he claimed), and prospected under the Australian sun. After impregnating a girl, he fled to New Zealand, where he quickly made a small fortune farming

flax. With a bank account amounting to more than $30,000, Oakes was now a wealthy man, and might have lived a very different life had his desire for gold not been so strong. He left New Zealand behind, again in pursuit of gold, and ended up in California's Death Valley, where he very nearly died of heat stroke. The winter of 1912, however, found Oakes suffering sub-zero temperatures at Kirkland Lake, Ontario. It was there, with the aid of the appropriately named Tough brothers, that Oakes finally struck gold. Greater success would come in 1918 with his Lake Shore Mines. The second largest gold find in North America, it earned Oakes approximately $60,000 each day. Within eight years he was considered the wealthiest man in Canada.

In 1923, at the age of 48, Oakes went back to Australia to marry Eunice MacIntyre, a beautiful woman who was half his age. The couple returned to Canada and, in their mansions at Kirkland Lake and the more temperate Niagara Falls, they raised a family of four children.

He renounced his American citizenship and became a naturalized Canadian. Through contributions to the federal Liberal party, he tried to buy his way into the Senate, but was stymied by the 1930 electoral victory of R. B. Bennett's Conservatives. As the Great Depression worsened, Oakes, the largest taxpayer in the Dominion, became convinced that the Bennett government was designing new tax laws as a punishment. He readily gave interviews with the press, in which his accusations were anything but veiled.

In 1934, Oakes left Canada for good, relocating his family to the first of several mansions in the Bahamas. As the colony's most wealthy resident, he developed his business empire – an airport, an airline, a hotel, a beachfront golf course and a country club – all the while devoting a potion of his wealth to worthy causes. For his efforts, he was created a baronet by George VI.

One dark cloud in Oakes' Caribbean paradise came in the form of the self-styled Count Marie Alfred Fouquereaux de Marigny. Known to his friends as Freddie, the twice-divorced count was known as something of a playboy. He enjoyed Nassau's social life and had been romantically attached to several women. It was therefore understandable that Oakes and his wife were not at all pleased when Freddie eloped with their eldest daughter, Nancy, shortly after her 18th birthday. There was no love lost between the father and his son-in-law. Their very public arguments soon became the talk of Nassau's upper crust.

Then, on 8 July 1943, Oakes was found murdered in his bed. He had been beaten about the head, doused with gasoline and set alight. The body was found by real estate promoter Sir Harold Christie, a long-time business associate, who had spent the evening in a guest room, two doors away from the scene of the murder. The surviving members of the Oakes family, Nancy included, were visiting the United States.

## He had been beaten about the head, doused with gasoline and set alight.

Speculation as to the identity of the murderer was quickly joined by talk of conspiracy. From the beginning, the Bahamian Governor, the Duke of Windsor, took charge of the investigation. It was an unprecedented step, made all the more unusual by the decision to disregard his own men and send for James Barker and Edward Melchen. Miami police detectives, they would earn the distinction of heading what is considered the most inept murder investigation in Bahamian history.

These two men, purportedly brought in as experts in the field of fingerprint identification, arrived from Florida without their equipment. They next made what seemed the most amateurish of errors: failure to secure the scene of the crime. After Oakes' charred body was removed, Barker and Melchen allowed members of the colony's gentry to visit the bedroom and handle its contents.

The day after the murder, the Miami detectives had Freddie de Marigny arrested, based on a fingerprint they claimed to have found at the crime scene. The Count was summarily charged with the murder of his father-

in-law. Nancy moved quickly in her husband's defence. She brought in her own detectives, who arrived at the Oakes mansion to find police officers scrubbing the walls of Sir Harry's bedroom. This loss of evidence was compounded by further bungling on the part of Barker. The detective had photographed the bedroom, capturing a bloody handprint near the bed, but allowed the negatives to be exposed to light before they could be developed. Meanwhile, the plane carrying Oakes' body for burial in Bar Harbor, Maine, was forced to return to Nassau after it was discovered that Barker and Melchen had failed to obtain the dead man's fingerprints.

Three months after his arrest, Freddie de Marigny went to trial at the Bahamas Supreme Court. His barrister, Godfrey Higgs, was not his first choice. In fact, the man he had hoped to use in his defence, Sir Alfred Adderley, had been recruited by the Crown to lead the prosecution.

Harold Christie, who was present in the mansion at the time of the murder, proved a poor witness. He claimed to have last seen Oakes alive shortly before midnight, when he retired for the evening. Christie had awoken during the night – not because of sounds of a struggle, but to swat away some pesky mosquitoes. Later still, he was drawn from his sleep by the sounds of the storm outside the guest room windows. It wasn't until he entered Oakes' bedroom the next morning that Christie noticed anything unusual. Thinking Sir Harry was still alive, he had cradled the dead man's head, attempting to give him water. After wiping Oakes' head with a towel, Christie had run out of the room, screaming for help.

In his questioning, Higgs attempted to swing suspicion away from his client and towards Christie. Why was it, the barrister wondered, that Oakes' business partner had parked his car so far from the house? Higgs called on the

Superintendent of the Bahamas Police Force who stated that he had spotted Christie in a car travelling away from the harbour shortly after midnight on the evening of the murder.

The prosecution, meanwhile, focussed on testimony from those who had witnessed the arguments between the victim and the accused.

The most interesting part of the trial occurred when the two Miami detectives took the stand, revealing an incompetence that bordered on the comical. Barker had claimed in the press that Freddie de Marigny had been arrested on the basis of a fingerprint found on a Chinese screen at the scene. Yet under oath Melchen revealed that it was six days later that he had been told of the identity of the fingerprint. This claim in itself contradicted an earlier statement that ten or eleven days had passed before he'd been aware that the fingerprint belonged to de Marigny.

Barker's testimony further discredited the efforts of the two detectives. He revealed that he had not obtained the fingerprint through usual methods, which involved dusting, photography

## Thinking Sir Harry was still alive, he had cradled the dead man's head, attempting to give him water.

and tape; rather, he had lifted the print using a piece of rubber, destroying the original in the process. When presented with the Chinese screen, he was unable to recall exactly where he had found the fingerprint.

Under Higgs' questioning, it was revealed that the detective had failed to look for fingerprints in key areas of the bedroom. Most damaging of all, after stating that he had obtained fingerprints of all who had visited the room, Barker was forced to reverse his claim and admit that he had not.

BELOW:
**The bloodied Chinese screen on which Freddie de Marigny's fingerprint was supposedly found.**

In the midst of this testimony, public mood, once so very much against Freddie de Marigny, switched to his side. When, on 12 November, de Marigny was found not guilty in the murder of his father-in-law, justice was seen to be done.

However, the question as to who killed Sir Harry Oakes remained. A more intriguing mystery was motive.

The victim's son-in-law had proposed that Oakes had for years been squirreling funds away in Mexico. He argued that Sir Harry's plan was to follow his money, leaving business partner Christie alone to deal with some rather dubious land deals.

De Marigny's premise was, perhaps, the least appealing to those attracted to conspiracy theories. For how might we explain the unusual moves made by the island's Governor, the Duke of Windsor? One theory has it that Sir Harry and the Duke were involved in money laundering, thus explaining the latter's intrusion in the murder investigation.

Another popular, though highly unlikely, hypothesis sees Oakes murdered by Axel Wenner-Gren, a friend of Hermann Goering, who, with the Duke of Windsor, was supposedly involved with a Nazi spy operation.

We are left only with theories, most of which involve one or more of the colony's prominent, slightly stained residents. The push to establish casinos on the island, opposed strongly by Oakes, is often cited as the reason for the murder. Harold Christie, for one, would have made a great deal of money had gambling come to the Bahamas. If this was, in fact, the motivation, others who might have participated include American mobsters Charles 'Lucky' Luciano and Meyer Lansky.

## SIR HARRY'S HIDDEN GOLD

LEFT:
The stately Oak Hall in Niagara Falls. Today it serves as the headquarters of the Niagara Parks Commission.

As befits a man of great wealth, Sir Harry Oakes owned several mansions. Of these, the most lavish was Oak Hall, built at Niagara Falls on a property he bought for half a million dollars in 1924. A 37-room Tudor-style baronial mansion, it was constructed over a period of four years, and is thought to feature paneling procured from Hampton Court. Oakes lived at Oak Hall for seven years, longer than at any one of his homes. He also had a house in London's Kensington Gardens and another English home on three square kilometers (800 acres) of woodland outside Sussex. There were two homes in Nassau and another two on the same street in Palm Beach. It is rumoured that each of these homes contains gold hidden between the walls.

# The Execution of Wilbert Coffin

There is no mystery as to who killed Wilbert Coffin. He was executed after having been found guilty of murder. However, half a century after his death the question remains as to whether he was an innocent man.

In July 1953, the bodies of three Americans from Altoona, Pennsylvania; 20-year-old Frederick Claar, 17-year-old Richard Lindsey and his father Eugene Lindsey, were found in the Gaspé Peninsula. Bear-hunters, they appeared to have been mauled by their prey. Clothing, scattered about their campsite, provided indications as to causes of death. These three men had not been killed by bears, but by firearm.

The state of the remains made the time of death extremely difficult to determine. The only expert to investigate concluded that the three men had died at some point before 18 June.

Wilbert Coffin, an illiterate woodsman and prospector was arrested and charged with the murders.

Born in 1915, Coffin was a likeable, generous man, though something of a loner. He'd spent most of his adult life in the bush, seeking riches through prospecting. Coffin's knowledge of the land led hunters to seek him out as a guide. It was this very skill that made him the prime suspect in the murders of the three Americans. Previous to his arrest, Coffin's only run-in with the law had come when he'd been caught hunting deer out of season.

The subsequent trial, for the murder of Richard Lindsey, was marked by incompetence and political interference. A considerable amount of documentation indicates that the Union Nationale government of Maurice Duplessis was demanding a quick resolution. Hunting and fishing brought a great deal of money to rural Quebec. It was a favourite destination of American sporting organizations, such

ABOVE:
**Wilbert Coffin was 40 years old when he was executed for murdering an American hunter.**

as the 200,000-strong membership of the Pennsylvania Federation of Sportsmen's Clubs. The Premier feared that the unsolved murder of three American hunters would have severe economic consequences for the area, and it could not have pleased Duplessis to learn that the Quebec Provincial Police had already been contacted by John Foster Dulles, the United States Secretary of State.

Noël Dorion, the prosecutor in the court case, was selected personally by the Premier, as was the lead detective, Alphonse Matte. Curiously, Quebec City lawyer Raymond Maher, a friend and supporter of Duplessis, turned up in Gaspé offering to represent Coffin.

RIGHT:
**The statue of Maurice Duplessis that stands outside Quebec's National Assembly.**

LEFT:
The imposing
building of Bordeaux
Prison in Montreal,
where Coffin was
hanged on 10
February 1956.

The Crown was unable to present a single eyewitness to the crime. Much of its case rested on the fact that Coffin had given the men a lift to a service station. The accused also had some of the Americans' belongings. However, Coffin was never permitted the opportunity to explain exactly how these items had come to be in his possession; after the Crown had presented its case, Maher stood and said, simply: 'The defence rests.' Although the lawyer, in his opening statement, had told the jury that he had travelled nearly 2,000 kilometres (1,200 miles) conducting interviews, he called none of the over hundred witnesses he said would be called upon to testify in the case. Not a single piece of evidence was called in support of the defendant, nor was Coffin given the opportunity to testify in his own defence.

In his closing address to the jury, the Crown prosecutor Noël Dorion stated: 'I have faith that you will set an example for your district, for your province and for the whole of your country before the eyes of America, which counts on you, and which has followed all of the details of this trial.'

After thirty minutes of deliberation, the jury returned a guilty verdict. Coffin received what was then the maximum sentence: death by hanging.

The story of this simple man who was given the harshest of penalties might have been forgotten had it not been for a group of dedicated lawyers who sensed injustice in the Gaspé.

What we know of Coffin's version of events comes through the 16 days of police interrogation following his arrest. Sitting in a rat-infested cellar, the guide had claimed that he'd met the three hunters on 10 June 1953, while beginning yet another prospecting trip. According to Coffin, the fuel pump on their truck had given up, so he gave Richard Lindsay a lift into town to buy a replacement. He later returned Lindsey to the camp, and was given 40 American dollars and a pocket knife for his trouble. Two days later, Coffin again drove to the camp, but found it deserted, except for the truck. The guide said that he waited several hours, before leaving with the broken fuel pump and a few clothes. He offered drunkenness as an explanation for the minor pilfering.

Coffin then left the bush for Montreal, where he stayed with his common-law wife, Marion Petrie. This fact should have presented a problem for the prosecution. A garage owner had seen two of the Americans during the time Coffin was in Montreal. Moreover, police had found a note dated 13 June that was written by one of the murder victims. However, Maher had failed to bring either of these issues to the attention of the jury.

In the 18 months that followed the conviction, Coffin received eight stays of execution. On 6 September 1955, his case took a bizarre, if clichéd twist, when he managed to escape from prison with the aid of a bar of soap carved into the shape of a gun. On the run, Coffin made the mistake of contacting Maher, who convinced his client to turn himself in. Just hours after his escape, Coffin had returned to prison, certain that his lawyer had been correct that the appeals process would find him innocent.

## He managed to escape from prison with the aid of a bar of soap carved into the shape of a gun.

His appeal made it all the way to the Supreme Court of Canada which, on 8 February 1956, upheld his conviction in a 5–2 decision.

One minute after midnight, on 10 February 1956, Coffin was hanged at the Bordeaux Prison in Montreal. Outside its walls, a crowd lining the shore of Rivière des Prairies prayed for his soul.

Despite Coffin's death, efforts continued to exonerate him. Journalist and publisher Jacques Hébert, a future senator, wrote two books in which he argued the dead man's innocence. While the first book, *Coffin était innocent*, raised the ire of Duplessis and his government, the second prompted a Commission of Inquiry. *J'accuse les assassins de Coffin* had the advantage of being published in 1963, during the Quiet Revolution. It was well received by many who saw political advantage in its harsh criticisms of Maurice Duplessis and his Union Nationale government. A 1964 Royal Commission

BELOW:
A pocketknife of the sort Coffin claimed he was given.

was established under Judge Raymond Brossard to rule out any wrongdoing and injustice in what had become known as *L'Affaire Coffin*. However, after listening to the testimony of more than 200 witnesses, the commission ruled that Coffin had indeed received due process and that the verdict had been just. Future prime minister Pierre Elliott Trudeau criticized the report, observing that Brossard had appointed Captain Jean-Charles Van Houtte, a chief investigator in the murders, to review the police investigation. The captain was amongst those whom Hébert had denounced in his books.

After the inquiry cleared the authorities, Hébert was sentenced to 30 days in prison and a $3,000 fine. He was, however, far from discredited. The Canadian public agreed with the author that something was amiss. Opinion polls indicated that most thought an innocent man had been executed. Those who fought successfully for the abolition of the death penalty often credit *L'Affaire Coffin* for having altered public opinion on the issue. Interestingly, evidence that has recently surfaced suggests that a man named Philippe Cabot was the murderer.

Wilbert Coffin, Frederick Claar, Richard Lindsey and Eugene Lindsey were not the only victims in *L'Affaire Coffin*: Marion Petrie had been refused permission to marry her common-law husband during his time in prison by none other than Maurice Duplessis himself. And then there was Sergeant Henri Doyon, head of the Quebec Provincial Police in the Gaspé, who was convinced that Coffin was innocent. He was demoted and, eventually, fired. Denied a pension after 25 years of service, Doyon suffered a nervous breakdown, turned to drink, and died a premature death.

While the murderer or murderers of the three American hunters may remain a mystery, others are certain of the man responsible for the death of Wilbert Coffin: Quebec Premier

## 'NOW I AM HELD TO BE A BLACK ASSASSIN'

The late Jacques Hébert had no qualms in describing Wilbert Coffin's execution as an 'assassination'. The motives behind the sentence, he argued in his books, were economic and political. By coincidence, Hébert knew and had published the work of another man who was the victim of assassination, Pierre Laporte. Kidnapped and strangled by terrorists during the October Crisis, the Vice-Premier and Minister of Labour of Quebec is one of only two politicians in Canadian history to have been felled by an assassin.

The other, Thomas D'Arcy McGee, was shot in the head from behind as he returned from Parliament during the early hours of 7 April 1868. Rumour quickly spread through Ottawa that the politician had been killed by a Fenian. It was the most obvious of theories. In the years leading to the assassination, the Fenians had made several incursions into Canada, and were still very much considered a threat. McGee, who had once fought strenuously against British North America, had come to apply even greater effort in working for Confederation. As such, he was considered by the Fenian Brotherhood to be the greatest traitor to their cause.

It is difficult to determine how many people were detained in the search for McGee's assassin – his biographer, T. P. Slattery, claims 'hundreds'. Whatever the number, amongst those picked up was a red-headed tailor by the name of Patrick James Whelan. He was carrying in his pocket a fully loaded .32 calibre Smith and Wesson Model 2 Army revolver – an expensive item, considered the most advanced of its day. On 9 April, the tailor was charged with McGee's murder.

Details of Whelan's life prior to his arrival in Canada remain remarkably elusive. It can be said with certainty that he was born in Ireland, yet the exact location and date are unknown. As a boy, it would appear that he was a tailor's apprentice. Whelan likely immigrated to Canada in 1865, and was probably in his mid twenties at the time.

After arriving in the country, he moved from job to job, working as a tailor for a man named Vallin in Quebec City; Gibb and Company in Montreal and; finally, Peter Eagleson in Ottawa. Contrary to the implications of this rather transitory existence, he was by all accounts skilled at his trade. He was known to frequent the visitor's gallery at the House of Commons.

After five months of sitting in prison, in September 1868 Whelan was finally put on trial before a jury at Ottawa's Court of Common Pleas. This man, thought to be a Fenian, had as his lawyer John Hillyard Cameron, Grand Master of the Orange Order. Prime Minister Sir John A. Macdonald, McGee's close friend, attended all eight days of the trial.

Whelan probably knew he was doomed. On the last day of the trial, he appeared in court dressed entirely in black. When the guilty verdict was read, he declared: 'Now I am held to be a black assassin. And my blood runs cold. But I am innocent. I never took that man's blood.'

There were appeals, but these were ultimately unsuccessful.

On 11 February 1869, at Carleton County Gaol, Whelan ascended the snow-covered steps of the scaffold and, turning to the crowd of 5,000 who had come to witness the execution, revealed that he knew the man who had killed Thomas

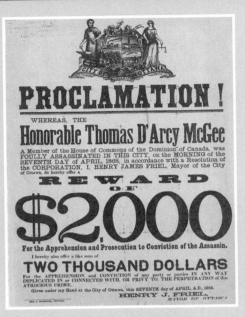

LEFT:
The reward offered for the assassin led to hundred of suspects being rounded up.

D'Arcy McGee. Assuming Whelan was telling the truth, he took the secret to his death. His hanging was the last public execution in Canada.

His body was transported to the back courtyard of the jail, where it was buried in an unmarked grave. Whelan's ghost is said to walk the grounds.

Curiously, the dead man's Smith and Wesson disappeared, only to turn up on the centenary of the assassination. Taking advantage of one hundred years of advances in criminal research methodology, ballistics experts conducted tests on the firearm; the results produced were inconclusive.

BELOW:
The funeral of Thomas D'Arcy McGee.

# The Suicide of E. Herbert Norman

Historians frequently describe the 12 years that followed the Second World War as the 'Golden Age' of Canadian diplomacy. It was a time when the Dominion, a country of between 13 and 16 million, had its greatest presence on the world stage. The climax of these labours, if they could be said that they had one, occurred at the end of 1957, when Lester B. Pearson was awarded the Nobel Peace Prize for his work in resolving the Suez Crisis. It was due largely to Pearson, aided through the great gathering of talent in the Department of External Affairs, that the first United Nations peacekeeping force was created. Though it was a grand achievement, celebration was tempered somewhat by the mysterious death eight months earlier of E. Herbert Norman, the Canadian Ambassador to Egypt. Early on the morning of 4 April 1957, Norman had stepped off the roof of a seven-storey building near his residence in Cairo.

Pearson, then Minister of External Affairs, spoke on the radio: 'I would like to say merely this, that the sense of shock and grief that I feel at the death of an old friend is made all the more bitter by the circumstances of his passing. He was a victim of persecution. He was also one of the finest, most loyal and most devoted public servants in the government of Canada, and we shall miss him very much. But let's not try to make an international incident out of this. Only one or two people in Washington persecuted him; the rest of them knew his worth.'

Opinion within the country held that Norman had been the victim of McCarthyism, in a particularly malicious campaign of smear and innuendo launched by the U.S. Senate Internal Security Subcommittee. Member of Parliament Alister Stewart went so far as

ABOVE:
**E. Herbert Norman,
the most gifted
Japanologist
of his day.**

to accuse the subcommittee of 'murder by slander'.

The suicide of Edgerton Herbert Norman brought a sudden, violent end to the career of a man who had been devoted to public service. His was in no way a typical Canadian story. Born on 1 September 1909 in Karuizawa, Japan, the future diplomat was the third and final child of Canadian Methodist missionaries. Norman's first teacher, his mother, started him off on an impressive academic career, which included studies at the University of Toronto, Cambridge and Harvard.

In 1940, not long after he joined the Department of External Affairs, Norman published *Japan's Emergence as a Modern State*, a book that remains a key work in Japanese Studies. That same year, he was assigned to Tokyo, where

he served as third secretary in the Canadian Legation. After the December 1941 bombing of Pearl Harbor, Norman was interned for several months, before being released and returned to Canada in a prisoner exchange.

With the end of the Second World War, he went back to Japan as the head of the Canadian Liaison Mission. Considered by many as the West's most accomplished scholar on Japanese history, politics and culture, Norman worked as an advisor to General Douglas McArthur, Supreme Commander for the Allied Powers in Japan. McArthur considered Norman 'the most valuable man we have', and yet exercised no influence when, in the autumn of 1950, the U.S. Senate Internal Security Subcommittee came forth with evidence it claimed showed

Norman was a Communist.

Norman was recalled from Japan and met with Pearson to discuss the allegations. The American Subcommittee believed that as a student at Cambridge and Harvard, Norman had attended a number of Marxist study groups. Indeed, he had encountered Guy Burgess, Anthony Blunt, Kim Philby and Donald Maclean, the four members of the infamous Cambridge Spy Ring, who would later be exposed as KGB agents. Norman was quite open about his associations and his participation in the study groups.

The Royal Canadian Mounted Police Security Branch, the forerunner of Canadian Security Intelligence Service, conducted a seven-week investigation, during which they found no evidence that would call Norman's loyalty into question. A related allegation, that he was a long-standing member of the Communist Party, also seemed without merit.

The diplomat having been cleared by the enquiry, Pearson was eager to demonstrate his confidence. In 1953, Norman was assigned to New Zealand, where he took up the post of High Commissioner. Three years later he became ambassador to Egypt, where he quickly distinguished himself as one of the finest observers. His skills for diplomacy appeared to be unparalleled – it was Norman who convinced Gamal Abdel Nasser, the President of Egypt, to accept Canadian peacekeepers in the Sinai.

By 14 March 1957, the question of Norman's loyalties seemed a long-resolved, dead issue. Therefore, it came as a shock to Norman, Pearson, the Department of External Affairs and the Canadian government, when that afternoon the American Internal Security Subcommittee released to the press records of its six-year-old hearings, including the discredited claims alleging Norman to be a Soviet agent.

Pearson filed a strongly worded protest, which caused the U. S. State

RIGHT:
Robert Morris, the man accused of having conducted a smear campaign against Norman.

LEFT:
Irene and Herbert Norman. They were married in 1935, shortly after the diplomat's graduation from Trinity College, Cambridge.

Department to renounce the accusations of the Subcommittee. Despite this, Subcommittee Chief Counsel Robert Morris continued a dogged pursuit of Norman. Within three weeks, the Canadian diplomat was dead.

On the day of the suicide, in a most unusual move, the Senate Subcommittee received unanimous condemnation from the floor of the House of Commons. Opposition leader John Diefenbaker rose to say that Norman had been victim of a witch-hunt.

Moving quickly to defend the Subcommittee, Morris held a press conference at which he read an unidentified report in which it was claimed that Norman had been recalled by Canada after connections to known Communists had been uncovered. That

same day he happily posed for photographers holding a newspaper that read: 'Envoy Accused as Red Kills Self'.

Indignation was soon joined by speculation and confusion. Much was made over a number of suicide notes Norman had left behind. Surely, it was thought, these would provide an indication as to why this accomplished individual felt the need to take his own life. On 5 April, the day after the suicide, the *Globe and Mail* printed what it claimed were two of Norman's suicide notes. Both were fabrications. Two weeks later, the *New York Daily News* added to the mystery by printing what was supposed to be the entire texts of two suicide notes. In both Norman stated that he could not reveal the true reasons for his suicide. These notes, too, were fake. The *Chicago Tribune* and the Hearst newspaper chain printed false reports that had Pearson admitting Norman was a Communist.

Pearson weathered the storm well. What had begun as the most unpleasant of years ended with his acceptance of the Nobel Peace Prize and his victory,

**Subcommittee Chief Counsel Robert Morris continued a dogged pursuit of Norman. Within three weeks, the Canadian diplomat was dead.**

just weeks later, in the campaign for a new leader of the Liberal Party. Six years after Norman's death, Pearson became the 14th Prime Minister of Canada, an office he held until his resignation in 1968.

Much of his few remaining years were spent composing his memoirs. His reminiscences about Herbert Norman's death reflect bitterness and loss. 'I am not sure,' he writes, 'but I think I followed the right course.'

A 1990 report prepared for the Department of External Affairs, using all documentation held by the department, as well as all relevant secret service files, uncovered no evidence that Norman had been a spy or a Soviet agent of influence. While he might have been described as a Marxist as a young man, Norman's political philosophy shifted over time; he was never a member of any Communist Party. Finally, the report concluded that it was likely Norman had committed suicide for the reasons stated in the notes left behind.

Peyton V. Lyon, who submitted the report, concluded by stating: 'Herbert Norman was loyal to the people of

**On 5 April, the day after the suicide, the *Globe and Mail* printed what it claimed were two of Norman's suicide notes. Both were fabrications.**

Japan, the land of his childhood. He was loyal to humanity, and to the pursuit of historical truth. He was loyal to himself; he never denounced the idealistic youth who misguidedly saw in Communism and the Soviet Union the only hope for civilised man. He was above all, loyal to his friends and to his country.'

There is an expression that is sometimes credited to Joseph McCarthy: 'If it looks like a duck, walks like a duck, and quacks like a duck, it's a duck.' Whether the anti-Communist actually coined the phrase has been a matter of some debate, however, it is known that he and those working under him held it to be true.

It would seem that Herbert Norman's great weakness was not that he was a spy, but that he apparently fit the profile of what McCarthy and other anti-Communists believed a Soviet agent to be.

## TWO OF HERBERT NORMAN'S SUICIDE NOTES

Herbert Norman left a number of suicide notes, including two addressed to his older brother Howard (1905–1987), a United Church minister. In the second note, which is also addressed to Howard's wife, Gwen, Herbert Norman mentions his sister Grace and his wife Irene.

*Dear Howie:*
*I am overwhelmed by circumstances & have lived under illusions too long. I realize that Christianity is the only true way. Forgive me because things are not as bad as they appear. God knows they are terrible enough — But I have never betrayed my oath of secrecy — But guilt by association as now developed has crushed me. I have prayed God's forgiveness if it is not too late.*
*Love*
*Herbert*

*Dear Howie & Gwen:*
*You have been much in my thoughts. It is too complicated to explain in a note — Irene some day will discuss it with you — I am completely innocent but a victim to forces bent on my destruction — no I haven't a persecution complex.*
*I dearly love you both and your family God bless you and save you from any troubled or tragic mishap — one in the family is enough — you must have faith in my complete innocence — despite the filth of slander and speculation that will appear. My Christian faith — never strong enough I fear, has helped to sustain me in these last days. This letter includes in its embrace you and all the youngsters — I write to Grace too — Irene is an angel help her.*
*Love — warmest love —*
*Herbert*

# CHAPTER 5:
# THE SUPERNATURAL & OTHERWORLDLY

# *La Corriveau* and her Cage

For generations, parents throughout Quebec used the image of *la Corriveau* as a means of keeping their children in line. Like the folkloric bogeyman, she was a supernatural, evil being. There was, however, a significant difference – *la Corriveau* had once lived.

She was born and baptized Marie-Josephte Corriveau on 14 May 1733 in the rural parish of Saint-Vallier in New France, the only surviving daughter of Joseph Corriveau and his wife Marie-Françoise. Her early years were spent on the successful family farm. Then, at the age of 16, she married a local man named Charles Bouchard, also a farmer. Bouchard died at the end of April 1760, leaving Marie-Josephte a young widow with three children. A little more than a year passed before she remarried. Her new husband, Louis-Helene Dodier, was yet another farmer from Saint-Vallier.

It was not a happy union. In January 1763, after roughly 18 months of marriage, Marie-Josephte claimed physical abuse when launching a petition for permission to leave her husband's home. The effort was unsuccessful and, ultimately, unnecessary – before the month was up, Dodier was found dead in his barn, with several injuries to the head. His passing was attributed to blows received from the hooves of his horses, and the body was buried without delay. Despite the official cause of death, dark rumour and speculation soon spread through the parish.

Many living in Saint-Vallier had witnessed very public displays of ill will between Joseph Corriveau, whom they knew to be a violent man, and his son-in-law. The two men had fought over rent and a horse in which they shared ownership. It was all too obvious that Marie-Josephte and her father had committed murder. Although there had been no witnesses, rumour had it that Joseph had killed his son-in-law by hitting him with a tool used to groom horses.

These serious allegations were raised during a period of great transition. Only a few years earlier, New France had fallen to the British. Justice in the former French colony was now being administered by the British Army. All the talk coming out of Saint-Vallier, a mere 30 kilometres (20 miles) downriver from Quebec City, encouraged local military authorities to begin an investigation into the death of the farmer.

On 29 March 1763, Marie-Josephte and Joseph Corriveau were put on trial before a court composed of twelve British military officers. The testimony presented before these men was wildly divergent and contradictory; it seemed no one in Saint-Vallier could agree on anything they had witnessed. Marie-Josephte added to the confusion by presenting three differing accounts of the hours that led up to the discovery of her late husband's body. The testimony given by her cousin, Isabella Silvain, was scattered, moving the court reporter to write in frustration: 'She delivered herself in so indistinct, incoherent, and Contradictory a manner that there was no possibility to take down same.'

Nevertheless, when the trial ended, 11 days later, the jury of military officers were convinced that Joseph had murdered his son-in-law with a dung fork. He was sentenced to hang. Marie-Josephte, who had been declared an accomplice, and Isabella, who was found guilty of perjury, were to each receive 60 lashes with a cat-o'-nine tails. The two women would have been branded as well, had it not been for Joseph's revelations.

## After describing how she killed her husband with a blunt hatchet as he slept, the accused woman was found guilty and condemned to hang.

On the evening before Joseph's scheduled execution, his confessor, a Jesuit superior named Augustin-Louis de Glapion, convinced the condemned man to reveal the truth. This he did, telling the military authorities that he'd been covering up for his daughter; he added that Marie-Josephte alone was responsible for the murder.

In a second trial, two weeks later, it was Marie-Josephte's turn to confess. After describing how she killed her husband with a blunt hatchet as he slept, the accused woman was found guilty and condemned to hang. The sentence further stipulated that after the hanging, Marie-Josephte's body would 'be hung in chains wherever the Governor shall think fit'. It was a unique sentence, one that displayed great ignorance on the part of those passing sentence. 'Hanging in chains', as it was known, was a gender-specific punishment; it had never before been applied to a female.

Joseph Corriveau not only escaped the hangman's noose, but also obtained a certificate of innocence. Some months later, he was pardoned by royal assent from George III.

It is likely that the murderess was hanged on 18 April, three days after having received her sentence, at Buttes-à-Nepveu, overlooking the Plains of Abraham. Her lifeless body was placed in a cage, which was then hung from a gallows erected by the roadside at Pointe-Lévy, opposite Quebec City, on the south shore of the St Lawrence River. Marie-Josephte's corpse was on display until 25 May, when it was removed by order from Governor James Murray.

Both body and cage were buried in the St-Joseph-de-la-Pointe-Lévy church cemetery. Whether the body was removed from its prison beforehand is unknown. When excavations uncovered the cage in the mid 18th century, it was said to contain only a thighbone. The cage itself was removed to the cellar of the church, from where it was later stolen.

It eventually turned up in the United States, where it was featured as part of a macabre display put together by the showman P. T. Barnum for his circus sideshow. In the early 20th century, Marie-Josephte's cage was on display at a Boston museum, where it was destroyed by fire.

In revealing the truth behind the murder of his son-in-law, Joseph Corriveau pointed out the obvious in stating that the testimony presented at his trial had been unreliable, confused and contradictory. Amongst those he mentioned by name as having delivered such testimony was labourer Claude Dion, who had lived with Marie-Josephte and her husband. Dion had a reputation as a great talker with a wild imagination and may be considered one of the earliest sources of the legends and stories about *la Corriveau*.

After Marie-Josephte was convicted of killing Louis-Helene Dodier, there was speculation that she had also

murdered her first husband. It came to be accepted that she had poured molten metal in his ear while he was asleep, and the gap in time between her two marriages was reduced from fifteen months to just three. As Marie-Josephte's legend grew, so did the number of husbands – at least one source places the number at seven. After her death, she became known as a poisoner, the preferred method of murderesses. In his 1877 novel *The Golden Dog*, William Kirby portrays Marie-Josephte as a direct descendant of Catherine Deshayes – *la Voisin* – the infamous 17th-century poisoner. Considered a sorceress, the connection between *la Voisin* and *la Corriveau* adds to the supernatural elements of the latter's legend.

During the five weeks it was hanging in the cage, *la Corriveau's* corpse is said to have reached through the rungs at passers-by, pleading to be taken to a

ABOVE LEFT:
**The gruesome fate of *la Corriveau*, the legendary murderess.**

Satanic celebration. Even after its removal, people of the area, fearing her ghost, avoided using the stretch of road on which the cage had been displayed. In some stories she is depicted as a witch, who somehow survived her hanging and subsequent imprisonment in the cage to torment the citizens of the parish.

*La Corriveau* is no longer seen along the south shore of the St Lawrence River. Accounts of her many appearances and guises have come to be appreciated as folk tales. Her mysterious supernatural abilities are dismissed as nothing more than entertainment or tools used by parents hoping to keep their children in line. Two and a half centuries after her execution, it just may be that Marie-Josephte Corriveau is finally at rest.

## JUSTICE UNDER GENERAL MURRAY

James Murray, the first Governor of Quebec, was not known as a particularly compassionate man. During his first months in the capital, before the surrender of the remainder of New France, he had three people hanged without trial. Until the restoration of French civil law with the passage of the 1774 Quebec Act, he oversaw a military court that handed out the harshest of sentences. A boy who had been convicted of robbery received 1,000 lashes for his crime. It could have been worse; the court explained that it had taken the age of the offender into account in handing down 'so mild a Punishment'.

The sentences brought down in the first trial in the murder of Louis-Helene Dodier provide a clear example of what Governor Murray considered a just sentence:

GENERAL MURRAY.

*Quebec, 10th April, 1763*

*GENERAL ORDER*
*The Court-martial, whereof Lt.-Col. Morris was president, having tried Joseph Corriveau and Marie Josephte Corriveau, Canadians, for the murder of Louis Dodier, as also Isabelle Sylvain, a Canadian, for perjury on the same trial, the Governor doth ratify and confirm the following sentence: That Joseph Corriveau having been found guilty of the charge brought against him, he is therefore adjudged to be hung for the same.*

*The Court is likewise of opinion that Marie Josephte Corriveau, his daughter, and widow of the late Dodier, is guilty of knowing of the said murder, and doth therefore adjudge her to receive sixty lashes, with a cat-o'-nine tails on her bare back, at three different places, viz: under the gallows, upon the market-place of Quebec and in the parish of St Valier; twenty lashes at each place, and to be branded in the left hand with the letter M.*

*The Court doth also adjudge Isabelle Sylvain to receive sixty lashes with a cat-o'-nine tails, on her bare back, in the same manner, and at the same time and places as Marie Josephte Corriveau, and to be branded in the left hand with the letter P.*

# The Headless Woman of Griffintown

Ask one of Montreal's younger residents for directions to Griffintown and one is likely to be met with a blank stare. They are to be forgiven. This rather sizeable area – stretching north and south from rue Notre-Dame to the Lachine Canal, and east and west between McGill and Guy streets – has been all but forgotten; its name does not feature on contemporary maps, nor is it mentioned in guidebooks. In Montreal, there are no street signs pointing to Griffintown, and yet this neighbourhood was once one of the most vibrant and important parts of the city.

The unskilled Irish labourers of Griffintown worked for the railways and at the harbour. They twice

BELOW:
**The Victoria Jubilee Bridge, commonly known as the Victoria Bridge, is 3 kilometres (1.8 miles) long. Completed in 1859, it was considered one of the great engineering marvels of its day.**

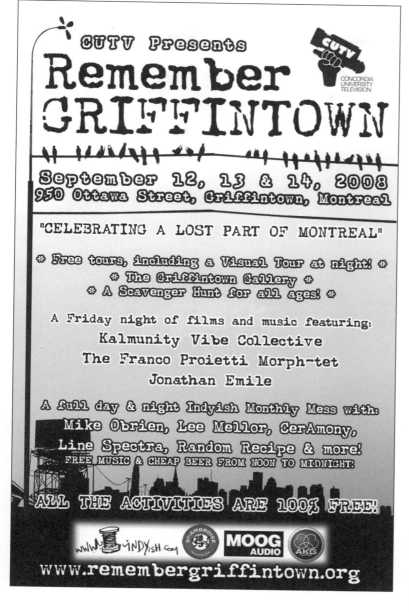

ABOVE:
**Recent years have seen a number of efforts to keep the Griffintown name alive.**

expanded the Lachine Canal, and built the Victoria Bridge, once considered the 'Eighth Wonder of the World'. The reward for this work was not great. Writing during the Second World War, economist and humorist Stephen Leacock described Griffintown as 'a wretched area, whose tumbled, shabby houses mock at the wealth of Montreal'.

It was during that same conflict that a RAF Liberator took off from Dorval,

## According to court documents, both women were 'known to police as loose and disorderly characters'.

experienced engine trouble, and slammed into a block of houses, killing 15 souls. This disaster came as Griffintown was about to enter its decline. Post-war, families began to leave. By 1963, the area had been rezoned for industrial use. Further destruction occurred a few years later with the building of the Bonaventure Expressway. In 1990, after nearly 170 years as Griffintown, the city renamed the neighbourhood Faubourg-des-Récollets, in honour of the first order of missionaries to settle in Montreal.

However, to those with an interest in the paranormal, the original name lives on through the ghost of Mary Gallagher – the Headless Woman of Griffintown.

The events leading to Mary Gallagher's beheading began on the afternoon of 26 June 1879, when the victim met with her best friend, Susan Kennedy. Though Gallagher and Kennedy where married women – to Messrs Connolly and Mears, respectively – each earned their living through prostitution. According to court documents, both women were 'known to police as loose and disorderly characters'. Contemporary newspapers aren't nearly so gentle, referring to Gallagher and Kennedy as 'dissipated characters…in the habit of having friends in to see them and of carrying on the most disgusting orgies.'

The two women went to Place Jacques-Cartier where they shared two bottles of whisky. As the afternoon turned to evening, the 38-year-old Gallagher managed to pick up a young man named Michael Flanagan. In the early hours of the next morning, all three returned to Kennedy's home, an upstairs flat in a tenement house at the corner of William and Murray streets. The hostess left briefly for yet another bottle of whisky, which Flanagan managed to share before passing out.

As he slept, the two women began bickering; the commonly held view is that Kennedy was jealous of her friend's beauty and success in picking up men. At some point, she grabbed an axe,

which she used to kill Gallagher. A ground-floor neighbour later testified that she'd heard a loud thud from the flat above her own, followed by more than ten minutes of what sounded like chopping.

It wasn't until the evening that police learned of the murder. They found most of Mary Gallagher lying on the floor – but her severed head and one hand had been placed in a washtub beside the stove. Rendered immobile by intoxication, Susan Kennedy lay covered in blood on a bed in the back room.

Both friend and client were charged with the murder. While Flanagan was acquitted, Kennedy's defence struggled on her behalf. They failed in an attempt to demonstrate insanity.

Kennedy was convicted of murdering her friend. Though the jury recommended mercy be shown, she was sentenced to hang on 5 December. It was the most shocking of decisions: to think that a woman would commit such a horrific crime was a shock to Victorian sensibilities.

Kennedy would have become the third Canadian woman to be executed had her sentence not been commuted by the Prime Minister, Sir John A. Macdonald. However, the date of the intended execution did not pass without a death. In a curious coincidence, on 5 December Michael Flanagan drowned in the Lachine Canal.

ABOVE:
**The Lachine Canal, in which Michael Flanagan was found drowned.**

RIGHT:
**Prime Minister Sir John A. Macdonald, who spared Kennedy the death sentence.**

In 1895, 16 years after the murder, Kennedy was released from prison, and returned to the neighbourhood of Griffintown, where she lived for the

## On the seventh anniversary of the murder, the headless, cloaked figure of Mary Gallagher was seen wandering about the neighbourhood.

remaining 11 years of her life. It is said that children would leave offerings of penny candy at her door in the hope that they would be spared her murderous wrath. For some parents, at

least, Kennedy's presence was used as a method to keep their sons and daughters in line.

Susan Kennedy died in 1916, but fear amongst the children of Griffintown continued due to an event that had taken place on 27 June 1886. On the seventh anniversary of the murder, the headless, cloaked figure of Mary Gallagher was seen wandering about the neighbourhood. From that day forward, at seven-year intervals, 27 June became known in Griffintown as Mary Gallagher Day.

For decades the children of Griffintown would avoid 242 William Street, the address of the crime. The local parish priest is said to have sprinkled holy water on the site. As late as 2005, Father Thomas McEntee, Chaplain of the Ancient Order of Hibernians, held a mass for the repose of Gallagher's soul.

Thus far, nearly two dozen sightings have been claimed, many having occurred on the same evenings, with the ghost variously described as wearing black ankle boots, a white petticoat and a red dress adorned with ribbon of green silk.

On the last Mary Gallagher Day, 27 June 2005, nearly 1,000 people gathered at the corner of William and Murray streets, but the murdered woman's ghost failed to appear. In fact, there have been no sightings in over eight decades.

Explanations for the ghost's absence are varied. Some believe it has something to do with the demolition of the murder scene. It may be that the good Father, who died in 2008, finally succeeded in laying the murdered woman's soul to rest. Some claim that the apparition had been seeking, and eventually found, her head. To many, the answer is a simple one: there is no such thing as ghosts.

However, those who do believe look toward 27 June 2012, when the headless ghost of Mary Gallagher is scheduled to reappear.

ABOVE:
The ghost of Mary Gallagher, as described by many of those who have seen her.

## CANADA'S HEADLESS GHOST

RIGHT:
The Banff Springs Hotel. Originally constructed in 1888, the hotel was rebuilt in 1920 after it was destroyed by fire.

While it might be argued that her's is the most famous, the ghost of Mary Gallagher is most certainly not the only Canadian apparition walking or floating around without a head. Nor is Mary Gallagher's headless state unique within the city of Montreal. A second headless ghost, that of a man carrying a blinding candle, has been seen haunting the Condos LeRoyer Saint-Claude at the corner of St Paul and St Sulpice streets in the oldest part of the city. The building was constructed in 2000 on the site of the original Hôtel Dieu hospital, which had been destroyed by fire over 300 years earlier. Records of this apparition stretch back to the 17th century, when patients reported seeing the ghost accompanied by the sounds of heavy shoes and a rolling bottle being kicked along the floor.

The ghost of another 17th-century figure, that of a French nun known only as Sister Marie, is said to haunt French Fort Cove in Northumberland County, New Brunswick. Local folklore holds that the pious woman asked that she be sent to the region in order to attend to the Acadians. Her charitable work had been rumoured to be funded by a large amount of money that she kept buried in a secret location. One dark night, walking alone after having assisted in the delivery of a baby, Sister Marie was confronted by an individual or individuals who demanded to know the location of the buried funds. When the nun refused their request she was beaten with such ferocity that her head was parted from the rest of her body. A variation has it that her assailants were sailors, and that one cut off her head, while the other threw it into the waters of the cove. According to both versions, the head was never found. Those who have encountered the nun's ghost report that she asks for help in locating her head, sometimes offering an award of 1,000 guineas. Others say that Sister Marie carries her head, pleading that it be buried with the rest of her body. This seemingly chaste spirit has a reputation of sneaking up on young lovers who have sought the privacy offered by the lands overlooking the cove.

At the other end of the country, just off Vancouver's Burrard Inlet, employees at the Canadian Pacific Railway yards have reported seeing an apparition known as the Headless Brakeman. The ghost is said to be that of a railway brakeman known as Hub Clark who, in 1928, fell off a freight car and into the path of a passenger train, which severed his head from his body.

The Scottish Baronial Banff Springs Hotel is known for having numerous ghosts, so it is perhaps not surprising that one is described as lacking its head. The Headless Bagpiper has been seen – but not heard – walking the Rob Roy Dining Room. Other ghosts at the hotel include a bride who fell to her death down the hotel staircase, a number of male spirits who are said to haunt both the men's and the women's cloakrooms, and that of a talented deceased bartender. Tellingly, perhaps, this last apparition only appears to tell select patrons that they have had too much to drink.

While the identity of the Headless Bagpiper is a mystery, not so the headless ghost that haunts the Avon River in Stratford. In November 1876, the body – but not the head – of a man named Henry Derry was discovered floating in a pine coffin. A medical student later admitted to having stolen the body from the local Catholic cemetery. Apparently, he required only the head in furthering his studies of anatomy.

LEFT:
A Headless Bagpiper is just one of many ghosts said to haunt the Scottish Baronial Banff Springs Hotel.

# The Shag Harbour UFO

Beginning in the early 1960s, as the centenary of Confederation drew near, communities around Canada were encouraged to undertake Centennial projects. Many saw an opportunity to construct new public buildings. As plans for new town halls, libraries and hockey arenas were being drawn up across the country, the people of St Paul, a small prairie town in Alberta, came up with the most unusual of ideas. Its grand Centennial project, one of more than 100 planned by the community, was a UFO landing pad. Constructed of concrete, it was officially opened on 3 July 1967 by Paul Hellyer, the Minister of National Defence, who flew in by helicopter specifically for the event. A sign erected beside the pad, states: 'The area under the World's First UFO Landing Pad was designated international by the Town of St Paul as a symbol of our faith that mankind will maintain the outer universe free from national wars and strife. That future travel in space will be safe for all intergalactic beings, all visitors from earth or otherwise are welcome to this territory and to the Town of St Paul.'

As Centennial projects went, the UFO landing pad was a whimsical departure from the norm, yet was very much in keeping with the celebrations that took place in the summer of 1967. And, in the autumn, as the weather began to cool in St Paul, news came that a UFO had appeared – not at the well-built landing pad, but 4,500 kilometres (3,000 miles) to the east in the small fishing village of Shag Harbour, Nova Scotia.

The first documented sighting of the UFO was reported in the early moonless evening of 4 October 1967 by Captain Pierre Charbonneau and First Officer Robert Ralph, two pilots on Air Canada flight 305 flying at an altitude of 400 metres (1,200 feet) over south east Quebec. They observed a large coloured object off their left wing slightly above their altitude. The object had been in their sight for several minutes when it appeared to experience a series of explosions. The pilots had begun to take evasive action when the UFO disappeared into some clouds.

At 9 pm, Leo H. Mersey, the captain of a fishing drag off the coast of Sambro Light, Nova Scotia, reported seeing four UFOs in a box pattern.

Perhaps the first person to see the UFO from land was a 12-year-old named Chris Styles, who lived in Dartmouth, 200 kilometres (120 miles) north of Shag Harbour on the Atlantic coast. At approximately 10 pm, Styles was preparing for bed when he glanced out his window. What he saw was a dim orange light moving along the shoreline. According to Styles, it was like nothing he had ever seen. He grabbed his coat and ran down to the waterfront for a better look. The orange light was emanating from a sphere that he estimated to be roughly 18 metres (60 feet) wide.

ABOVE:
**A dramatic illustration of the account of fisherman Leo H. Mersey, who reported seeing four UFOs in a square formation.**

An hour later, at Shag Harbour, at least 16 people saw a low-flying object, approximately 20 metres (65 feet) in length, displaying four or five amber lights descending at a 45-degree angle over the harbour. It appeared to crash approximately 300 metres (100 feet) from the coast and then simply float on the surface of the water.

Calls from Bear Point, Cape Sable Island immediately poured into the regional headquarters of the Royal Canadian Mounted Police, reporting what all believed to have been the crash of an airplane. Fifteen minutes later, the Mounties arrived at the scene, in time to observe what appeared to be a pale light floating on the surface of the harbour. As a rescue mission was being assembled, the light sank below the surface.

Two fishing boats, launched in search of possible survivors, found nothing but a long streak of gold-coloured foam

most interesting of the related documents that are accessible to the public advised that a 'dark object' had crashed in Shag Harbour. Seven witnesses were named, including the presiding RCMP officer.

On 6 October, a team of Navy divers from the fleet diving unit in Halifax arrived at Shag Harbour. The divers sectioned off what was roughly a two kilometre (1.5 miles) by one kilometre (0.5 miles) area and began a search in the murky waters.

As the divers began their search, lighthouse keeper Ervin Banks claims that he found a partially burnt cylinder approximately a metre (3 feet) long and half a metre (1.5 feet) in diameter on the shore of Bonne Portage Island. According to Banks, he notified the Department of Transportation, who told him to wrap the object and deliver it to an American naval officer at nearby Prospect Point wharf. Banks says that he was told the man flew in from Virginia to pick up the cylinder.

Two days after the UFO sighting, Shag Harbour, a community of just a few hundred people, was now the subject of national news coverage. Those sent to cover the story met with frustration. No planes had been reported missing, nothing had fallen off the radar screens and the divers were finding nothing. Then, Ray MacLeod, a reporter from the *Chronicle-Herald* in Halifax, caught a break. He managed to get a phone interview with the head of the Royal Canadian Air Force Air Desk, Squadron Leader William Bain, during which the officer said that there might be, 'something concrete' to the incident. The following day, the headline of the *Chronicle-Herald* bore the headline: 'COULD BE SOMETHING CONCRETE IN SHAG HARBOUR UFO: RCAF'.

That same day, three additional divers were sent to the site. However, on 8 October, the search of the bottom of the harbour was terminated. According to the final report no trace of the mysterious object was found.

floating on the surface of the water. The Canadian Coast Guard, which arrived at the site just over an hour after the crash, also found nothing.

The next morning, after it was determined that all private, commercial and military aircraft in the area were accounted for, the Canadian Forces Headquarters was informed of the crash in a priority telex issued by the Rescue Co-ordination Centre in Halifax. Labelled 'UFO Report', this first and

The abrupt cancellation of the search, with no explanation offered, prompted rumour. There were some in the community who suspected a cover-up. There had been times when the divers had been spotted bringing things up from the bottom of the harbour. One story had it that an unnamed diver had admitted he'd brought something to the diving vessel – an object that he'd taken care to wrap while it was still underwater.

As rumours and speculation grew, Ray MacLeod was pulled off the story by his editor at the *Chronicle-Herald*. The reporter who replaced him, David Bentley, seemed intent on playing down the notion that the object that had crashed in Shag Harbour was a UFO. One of his chief sources was astronomer Father Michael Burke-Gaffney, Canada's pre-eminent UFO sceptic. A Jesuit priest, Burke-Gaffney was adamant that UFOs did not exist, and stated as much in a lecture he delivered within weeks of the Shag Harbour incident.

According to Ray MacLeod, when he asked Bentley why he wasn't following up with Squadron Leader Bain, the reporter responded that he had been told that Bain did not exist.

As the search had been taking place at Shag Harbour, several witnesses had observed a flotilla of Canadian and American ships off the coast of Shelburne, approximately 40 kilometres (25 miles) northeast of Shag Harbour. At the time, Shelburne was officially an oceanographic institute, but in reality the facility was a top-secret listening post set up to detect and track Soviet submarines.

One military witness, who has chosen to remain anonymous, has claimed that the object had first been detected on radar as coming out of Siberia. This account has the object sinking in Shag Harbour, then being tracked underwater by sonar, before coming to rest on a submarine magnetic detection grid. According to the witness, the UFO was then joined by another object, which appeared to lend assistance to the first. The flotilla was composed of Canadian and American ships, which monitored the two objects for a week. On 11 October, the flotilla left the site, apparently to intercept a Soviet submarine that had been detected coming into Canadian waters.

The story provided by the military witness – and the direction from which the UFO came – may imply that whatever landed at Shag Harbour was technology developed during those Cold War times. However, an American diver involved in the search claimed that the object he saw was alien. Identified only as 'Harry', the witness claimed that some foam-like debris was salvaged.

> **After ten minutes, it disappeared briefly, then reappeared lit by four orange lights. An hour later, its light now glowing yellow, it ascended into the night sky, vanishing for good.**

In Harry's account, the search was cancelled abruptly on the evening of 11 October when the UFO unexpectedly departed from a location close to the original Shag Harbour crash site.

If true, the calling off of the search is likely related to an event witnessed that same evening by Lockland Cameron and his family at Woods Harbour, one kilometre (0.5 miles) to the north of the original crash site. On 12 October, the *Chronicle-Herald* ran a story concerning the sighting of a seemingly identical UFO departing the area the previous evening, exactly one week after the initial crash. Cameron said that at approximately 10 pm, he and his family had witnessed an object roughly 18 metres (60 feet) in length with six bright red lights, at an altitude of about 150 metres (500 feet). After ten minutes, it disappeared briefly, then reappeared lit by four orange lights. An

ABOVE:
**Shag Harbour has become a popular tourist destination for those interested in UFOs.**

hour later, its light now glowing yellow, it ascended into the night sky, vanishing for good.

If the accounts provided by military witnesses are correct, the Shelburne search was much larger, longer and more concentrated than that which had taken place at Shag Harbour – yet only the latter has been officially documented.

Curiously, no Royal Canadian Mounted Police reports of the initial Shag Harbour sighting survive; however, the event is covered in several dozen unreleased official documents, three of which involve the Royal Canadian Air Force. The first is the aforementioned 5 October 'UFO Report' telex sent to Canadian Forces Headquarters by the rescue centre in

Halifax. The second is a telex to Canadian Maritime Command from Squadron Leader William Bain – the man who it was claimed did not exist – at the Royal Canadian Air Force Air Desk. In the communication Bain advises an immediate underwater search of the area. This was followed by a third telex, issued from Canadian Maritime Command to Fleet Diving Unit Atlantic, in which the latter was instructed to provide a diving officer and three divers for the search.

Four decades later, the Canadian Department of National Defence officially considers the sightings at Shag Harbour to be unsolved.

Typically, sightings of UFOs are held up as evidence that Earth is being visited by extraterrestrials. However, this is not necessarily the case to those who have studied the incident at Shag Harbour. There has been considerable speculation that what witnesses saw was the crash of a Soviet spacecraft. This would explain the apparent appearance in Canadian waters of a Soviet submarine just a few days later. Others have countered that the mysterious object was not Soviet, but American. Either possibility would explain the heavy American naval presence that followed the crash.

More than four decades after the event, the Shag Harbour incident has the distinction of being both the best documented UFO case in Canadian history and one of the country's greatest mysteries.

## DEPARTMENT OF NATIONAL DEFENCE MEMO

**Library and Archives Canada holds numerous pieces of official documentation concerning the Shag Harbour UFO, including this memo, dated the day of the crash, issued by the Department of National Defence:**

*UFO REPORT*
*LOWER WOOD HARBOUR, N.S.*

*An RCMP Corporal and six other witnesses observed what they believed to be an unidentified flying object off the south-west coast of Nova Scotia, Canada on the 4th October 1967. The object was described as approximately 60 feet [20 metres] in length and was flying in an easterly direction when first sighted. During their observation, the UFO descended rapidly to the surface and made a 'bright splash' as it struck the water. For some time after the impact a single white light remained on the surface. The RCMP Corporal endeavoured to reach the floating white object, but unfortunately, before he could reach the location the object sank. A search of the area failed to produce any material evidence which could assist in explaining or establishing the identity of the object. An underwater search conducted by divers from the Department of National Defence also failed to locate any tangible evidence which could be used to arrive at an explainable conclusion.*

ABOVE LEFT:
**Divers from the Deparment of National Defence searched the area for clues as to the identity of the sunken UFO.**

# BIBLIOGRAPHY

Arment, Chad. *The Historical Bigfoot: Early Reports of Wild Men, Hairy Giants, and Wandering Gorillas in North America.* Lancaster, PA: Coachwhip, 2006

Aubert de Gaspé, Phillipe. *Seigneur D'Haberville.* Toronto: Musson, 1929

Beattie, Owen, and John Geiger. *Frozen in Time: Unlocking the Secrets of the Franklin Expedition.* Saskatoon: Western Producer Prairie, 1992

Bell, Don. *The Man Who Killed Houdini.* Montreal: Véhicule, 2004

Berton, Pierre. *My Country: The Remarkable Past.* Toronto: McClelland & Stewart, 1976

Bocca, Geoffrey. *The Life and Death of Harry Oakes.* London: Weidenfeld & Nicolson, 1959

Bogle, Lori Lyn, ed. *The Cold War.* New York: Routledge, 2001

Bryce, George. *The Remarkable History of the Hudson's Bay Company.* Toronto: Briggs, 1900

Brightman, Robert A. 'Windigo in the Material World.' *Ethnohistory* 35:4 (Fall 1988). 337–379

Cartier, Jacques. *The Voyages of Jacques Cartier.* Toronto: University of Toronto Press, 1993

Cavanaugh, Catherine Anne, *et al. Alberta Formed, Alberta Transformed.* Edmonton: University of Alberta Press, 2006

Champlain, Samuel de. *Voyages of Samuel de Champlain.* Boston: The Prince Society, 1878

Collard, Edgar Andrew. *All Our Yesterdays.* Montreal: The Gazette, 1990

Colombo, John Robert. *Canadian Literary Landmarks.* Toronto: Dundurn, 1984

– *Ghost Stories of Canada.* Toronto: Dundurn, 2000

– *Mysteries of Ontario.* Toronto: Dundurn, 1999

– *Strange But True: Canadian Stories of Horror and Terror.* Toronto: Dundurn, 2007

Crooker, William S. *Oak Island Gold.* Halifax: Nimbus, 1993

Cyriax, Oliver. *Crime: An Encyclopedia.* London: André Deutsch, 1993

d'Artigue, Jean. *Six Years in the Canadian North-West.* Toronto: Hunter Rose, 1882

Daegling, David J. *Bigfoot Exposed: An Anthropologist Examines America's Enduring Legend.* Lanham, MD: Altamira, 2004

Donaldson, William. *Brewer's Rogues, Villains, and Eccentrics: An A–Z of Roguish Britons Through the Ages.* London: Cassell, 2004

'The Donnelly Massacre'. The *St Marys Argus*, 4 February 1880

Fanthorpe, Lionel and Patricia. *The World's Most Mysterious Murders.* Toronto: Hounslow, 2003

Fazarkas, Ray. *The Donnelly Album.* Toronto: Firefly, 1993

Fay, Charles Eden. *The Mystery of the 'Mary Celeste'.* New York: Dover, 1988

Fetherling, Douglas. *The Gold Crusades: A Social History of Gold Rushes, 1849–1929.* Toronto: Macmillan, 1988

Fetherling, George. *A Biographical Dictionary of the World's Assassins.* Toronto: Random House Canada, 2001

Fitterman, Lisa. 'Montreal Priest Never Forgot His Roots – or the Ghost of Mary Gallagher.' The *Globe & Mail*. 18 June 2008

Francis, Daniel. *The Imaginary Indian: The Image of the Indian in Canadian Culture.* Vancouver: Pulp, 1992

– *National Dreams: Myth, Memory, and Canadian History.* Vancouver: Arsenal Pulp, 1997

– *The Encyclopedia of British Columbia.* Madeira Park, BC: Harbour, 2000

Friscolanti, Michael. 'Atlantic Treasure'. *Maclean's*, 16 October 2006

Gravenor, Kristian. *Montreal: The Unknown City.* Vancouver: Arsenal Pulp, 2003

# BIBLIOGRAPHY

Greenwood, F. Murray, and Beverlet Boissery. *Uncertain Justice: Canadian Women and Capital Punishment, 1754–1953*. Toronto: Dundurn, 2000

Halpin, Marjorie M. and Michael M. Ames, eds. *Manlike Monsters on Trial: Early Records and Modern Evidence*. Vancouver: University of British Columbia Press, 1980

Hébert, Jacques. *J'accuse les Assassins de Coffin*. Montreal: Editions de Jour, 1963

Ho, Oliver. *Mutants and Monsters*. New York: Sterling, 2008

'The Inquest'. The *St Marys Argus*, 12 February 1880

Johnston, Sheila, M. F. *Let's Go to the Grand!: 100 Years of Entertainment at London's Grand Theatre*. Toronto: Dundurn, 2001

Kafla, Louis A. *Violent Crime in North America*. Westport, CT: Greenwood, 2003

Kane, Paul. *Wanderings of an Artist Among the Indians of North America: From Canada to Vancouver's Island and Oregon, Through the Hudson's Bay Company's Territory and Back Again*. London: Longman, Brown, Green, Longmans, and Roberts, 1859

Kearney, Mark. *The Great Canadian Trivia Book 2*. Toronto: Dundurn, 1998

Krantz, Grover S. *Bigfoot Sasquatch: Evidence*. Surrey, BC: Hancock House, 1999

Le Moine, James MacPherson. *Maple Leaves: A Budget of Legendary, Historical, Critical, and Sporting Intelligence*. Toronto: Hunter Rose, 1863

Leacock, Stephen. *Montreal: Seaport and City*. New York: Doubleday, Doran, 1944

Lenik, Edward J. *Picture Rocks: American Indian Rock Art in the Northeast Woodlands*. Lebanon, NH: University Press of New England, 2002

Lyon, Peyton V. 'The Loyalties of E. Herbert Norman.' *Labour/Le Travail*, 28 (Fall 1991): 219–221

MacGregor, Roy. 'The Legend,' The *Canadian*, 15 October 1977

Massey, Raymond. *When I Was Young*. Toronto: McClelland & Stewart, 1976

Miller, Orlo. *The Donnellys Must Die*. Toronto: Prospero, 2001

Morgan, Henry J., ed. *Dominion Annual Register and Review 1879*. Ottawa: MacLean, Roger & Co., 1880

Mowat, Farley. *Westviking: The Ancient Norse in Greenland and North America*. Toronto: McClelland & Stewart, 1965

'A Murder Horror!' The *St Marys Argus*, 5 February 1880

Murray, Joan. *Tom Thomson: Design for a Canadian Hero*. Toronto: Dundurn, 1998

Nickell, Joe. *Real-life X-files: Investigating the Paranormal*. Lexington, KY: University Press of Kentucky, 2001

North, Dick. *The Mad Trapper of Rat River: A True Story of Canada's Biggest Manhunt*. Guilford, CT: Globe Pequot, 2005

Ondaatje, Michael. *In the Skin of a Lion*. Toronto: McClelland & Stewart, 1987

Pearson, Lester B. *Mike: The Memoirs of the Right Honourable Lester B. Pearson, Volume Three*. Toronto: University of Toronto, 1975

Radford, Benjamin, and Joe Nickell. *Lake Monster Mysteries: Investigating the World's Most Elusive Creatures*. Lexington, KY: University Press of Kentucky, 2006

Sawatsky, John. *For Services Rendered: Leslie James Bennett and the RCMP Security Service*. Markham, ON: Penguin, 1983

'Senators Defend Right to Probe.' The *Globe & Mail*, 5 April 1957: 1–2

Slattery, T. P. *The Assassination of D'Arcy McGee*. Toronto: Doubleday Canada, 1968

Smith, Barbara. *Ghost Stories of Alberta*. Toronto: Dundurn, 1996

Strain, Kathy Moskowitz. *Giants, Cannibals and Monsters: Bigfoot in Native Culture*. Surrey, BC: Hancock House, 2008

Underhill, Doug. *Miramachi Tales Tall and True*. St John: Neptune, 1999

'Was the Wrong Man Hanged?' The *Gazette* (Montreal), 16 August 2006

# INDEX

# PICTURE CREDITS